THOMAS ROTHER

Britain Before the Reform Act: Politics and Society 1815–1832

Eric J. Evans

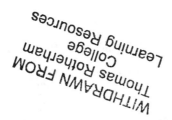

LONGMAN
London and New York

941.07 EVA

Addison Wesley Longman Limited
Edinburgh Gate, Harlow,
Essex CM20 2JE, England
and Associated Companies throughout the world.

Published in the United States of America
by Addison Wesley Longman Publishing, New York

First published 1989
Seventh impression 1996

Set in 10/11 point Baskerville Linotron
Produced through Longman Malaysia, CL

ISBN 0 582 00265-6

British Library Cataloguing in Publication Data

Evans, Eric J. (Eric John), *1945–*
   Britain before the Reform Act: politics
   and society, 1815–1832.—(Seminar studies
   in history).
   1. Great Britain. Political events, 1714–
   1837
   I. Title   II. Series
   941.07

   ISBN 0-582-00265-6

Library of Congress Cataloging in Publication Data

Evans, Eric J.
   Britain before the Reform Act, politics and society
   1815–1832.

   (Seminar studies in history).
   Bibliography: p.
   Includes index.
   1. Great Britain—Politics and government—1800–1837.
   I. Title. II. Series.
   DA535.E86   1989   941.07   88-13202
   ISBN 0-582-00265-6

Contents

Contents

Seminar Studies in History
Founding Editor: Patrick Richardson

Introduction

The Seminar Studies series was conceived by Patrick Richardson, whose experience of teaching history persuaded him of the need for something more substantial than a textbook chapter but less formidable than the specialised full-length academic work. He was also convinced that such studies, although limited in length, should provide an up-to-date authoritative introduction to the topic under discussion as well as a selection of relevant documents and a comprehensive bibliography.

Patrick Richardson died in 1979, but by that time the Seminar Studies series was firmly established, and it continues to fulfil the role he intended for it. This book, like others in the series, is therefore a living tribute to a gifted and original teacher.

Note on the System of References:
A bold number in round brackets (**5**) in the text refers the reader to the corresponding entry in the Bibliography section at the end of the book. A bold number in square brackets, preceded by 'doc'. [**doc. 6**] refers the reader to the corresponding item in the section of Documents, which follows the main text.

ROGER LOCKYER
General Editor

Part One: The Background

1 1815 and All That

1815 is an important date in British history. On 18 June in that year the Duke of Wellington, with vital help from the Prussian army at a late stage, defeated Napoleon Bonaparte, Emperor of France. The battle of Waterloo, fought just south of Brussels on the road to Paris, ended Napoleon's phenomenal military and political career. The 67,000 troops who fought under Wellington's command in the bloody, decisive engagement seemed to have settled the fate of Europe. They had ended the longest war in which Britain had been engaged since the fifteenth century and the most costly war yet fought. Britain's victory over the French gave her a commanding influence in European diplomacy which would not be lost for over a century.

Britain was the only nation which had kept up the European fight against first revolutionary, then Napoleonic, France from the time it entered the war in February 1793 to its end, with only a brief truce in 1802–3. Britain, alone among the significant European powers, had not been defeated or overrun by French armies. From being commercially important but nevertheless on the fringes of European affairs in the late eighteenth century, Britain was acknowledged in 1815 as the leading power in Europe and thus in the world. It is not surprising that many examination syllabuses follow Britain's development through her century of diplomatic, commercial, industrial and, latterly, imperial pre-eminence until the outbreak of the First World War in 1914.

In many ways, however, 1815 is an altogether less significant date. No new government took office in Britain then, and the end of the French wars marked no important change in Britain's domestic political affairs. When Wellington won the battle of Waterloo, the Earl of Liverpool had been Prime Minister for exactly three years. He led a Tory government, most of whose important members had come to political maturity during the earlier phase of the French Wars, and whose guiding principle had become opposition to reform for fear of opening the way to a British revolution.

The new Tory party had effectively been created as a coalition of anti-reforming land and other property owners under the younger Pitt in 1794, though Liverpool was the first Prime Minister of the period to acknowledge the description 'Tory'. The Tories had a secure majority in the House of Commons. The only non-Tory ministry to be formed between 1794 and 1830 – the so-called but hopelessly misnamed 'Ministry of all the Talents' – lasted only a year. Liverpool had become Prime Minister after the assassination of Spencer Perceval and, although his ministry had endured several early crises, he proved to be a great political survivor and was only removed from office by an incapacitating stroke early in 1827. Liverpool is far from being the best-known or most distinguished of British Prime Ministers, but he had many modest virtues. He was both dully competent and completely trust-worthy. He was, as Charles Long, one of the junior ministers he inherited from Perceval, asserted, 'one of the best tempered men living' (**19**). More talented but fractious colleagues would work with him when they would not co-operate with others. By 1827, he seemed not only irremovable but irreplaceable. As we shall see (Chapters 13 and 14) the Tory party could not replace him without breaking up. Liverpool's has proved to be by some distance the longest Prime Ministership in the nineteenth and twentieth centuries.

The monarchy, which still possessed separate and distinctive powers in Britain in the early nineteenth century, did not change hands in 1815. The King had in 1801 dismissed William Pitt the Younger (a popular, even revered, Prime Minister with a strong parliamentary majority) because he disagreed with him on an important issue of policy. Yet he did not create a constitutional crisis in so doing. The monarch remained the most important influence in the choice of every Prime Minister between the 1720s and the 1820s. The wishes of the House of Commons and the House of Lords were only factors the monarch was wise to take into account; those of the electorate mattered not at all. Yet as the right of the King to appoint his favourites to sensitive or influential positions by a system of 'patronage' was whittled away at the end of the eighteenth century, so royal power began to decline (**10**).

King George III had been on the throne since 1760 but his dull, dutiful demeanour had given way to progressive mental instability. 'Farmer George' began talking to the trees at Windsor Castle and, after various bouts of intellectual collapse, he was declared permanently unfit to govern in February 1811, whereupon his eldest son took over as Prince Regent. Prince George, who became King as George IV in 1820, though a man of some aesthetic sensibility, was vain, spiteful, gross and profligate. He was also politically incompetent, never understanding the distinction between a petulant outburst (of which he made many) and a firm statement (of which, though he thought differently, he made very few). While he was regent or monarch from 1811 to 1830, the remaining powers of the monarchy ebbed even more rapidly. It is probably true that George III mad had greater respect from his subjects than George IV sane. Rarely, in the chequered history of the British monarchy, has a King been so vilified.

There is a more fundamental reason why 1815 needs to be placed in a broader context. At the time, parts of Britain were being rapidly industrialised. Historians now agree that industrial revolutions transform societies much more fundamentally than does any political or diplomatic 'revolution'. Many of the crises with which this book is concerned were part of the early consequences of the Industrial Revolution, and a study which begins its detailed treatment in 1815 must show awareness of the transformations which affected Britain from the 1780s onwards. No one date can be selected to mark the beginning of the Industrial Revolution, but 1815 has no claim to be considered important in this wider industrial and social context.

Since the Industrial Revolution eventually transformed not only British society but its political system, political and social history in this period should be studied together in order to make sense of developments. It is a great gain in historical understanding that political historians now develop their arguments within a social framework (**5, 14, 20, 31, 76**). For their part, social historians have paid considerable attention to political struggles between the classes, especially over parliamentary reform in the early years of the nineteenth century (**4, 7, 40, 60, 77, 93**).

2   A Changing Society

British society was under great strain between 1815 and 1832 largely because of the speed of change. At the most basic level, it was getting bigger all the time. After a period of stagnation in the early eighteenth century, population began to grow steadily from the 1730s and with great rapidity from the 1780s. At the time of the first official census in 1801, the population of Britain was about 10.6 million, almost double its level a century earlier. In the mere seventeen years covered by this book it increased by almost 29 per cent from an estimated 12.9 million to 16.6 million. British population never grew faster than in the twenty years after 1811.

As those who study developing countries in our own time are well aware, rapid population increase is almost invariably accompanied by social dislocation. Britain in the early nineteenth century was indebted to an efficient domestic agricultural system and a well-developed pattern of overseas trade for the simple fact that very few of her population starved. But dislocation manifested itself in other ways. Rapid fluctuations in food prices lay behind much of the unrest of the period 1815–20. The average price of wheat, on which the Englishman's staple food of bread was based, was never higher in the whole of the nineteenth century than in the decade 1810–19, and prices rarely fluctuated as bewilderingly.

Another aspect of population growth has received less attention but is at least equally important. Britain's was a young population. Birth-rates were extremely high, largely because women were marrying earlier. This they were able to do because of increased job opportunities in a rapidly expanding economy. On average, in the first half of the eighteenth century, women in England got married for the first time at the age of 26.2 years. In the first half of the nineteenth century, this had fallen to 23.4 years (**49**). Given the limited number of years in which women are highly fertile, such a change is dramatic in its consequences. It has been estimated that no less than 48 per cent of the population of England and Wales in 1821 was less than fifteen years of age. Such a skewed distribution towards the very young placed enormous burdens on income earners and contributed to the desperation of much of the 'hunger politics' of this period. It is also worth considering to what extent protest movements are dependent upon the active participation of teenagers and young adults for their mass appeal. A population containing an unusually large proportion of young folk in it is inherently less stable than one in which the distribution is more even.

The more common picture of change in early industrial Britain concentrates on urban growth, factory production and on working conditions dominated allegedly by William Blake's 'dark, satanic mills'. No one doubts that the industrial revolution involved factories and the emergence of more specialised patterns of work in which human labour might be subordinated to the arbitrary rhythms of the machine. Nor is it to be denied that most factories (though not the earliest, which were water-powered and necessarily located in rural valleys next to fast-flowing streams and rivers) were found in towns. The Industrial Revolution and urban growth went hand in hand. It is important to remember four points about this development, however.

Firstly, the Industrial Revolution took place over a much longer time than is frequently assumed. In this period, factory production was almost exclusively concentrated on the manufacture of cheap textile goods, firstly cottons, then woollens. This took place in three areas of Britain: south-east Lancashire and north-east Cheshire; the central valley of Scotland; and Yorkshire's West Riding. Here grew up the great factory towns of early industrial Britain: Manchester, Bolton, Salford, Stockport, Glasgow, Paisley, Leeds, Bradford and the rest. Secondly, these factory towns were by no means dominated by monster factories employing thousands of workers in vast, impersonal surroundings. In 1841, only 3 per cent of cotton firms in Lancashire, the county of greatest factory concentration, employed more than 1,000 workers; 43 per cent employed fewer than 100 (**86**). The scale of early industrial production has generally been over-estimated.

Thirdly, much urban growth in the first half of the nineteenth century resulted from an expansion and consolidation of traditional methods, rather than from factory production. Birmingham, the centre of the west midlands metal trades and Sheffield, its counterpart in south Yorkshire, both doubled their populations in the first thirty years of the nineteenth century, a faster rate of growth than many textile towns. Yet both towns teemed with workshops owned by small master-manufacturers who employed skilled craftsmen, journeymen and apprentices as in the eighteenth century. The scale, not the nature, of such towns had changed. Urban growth did not require factory production, and it is worth recalling that one of the fastest urban growth rates in the decade 1821–31 was recorded on the Sussex coast by Brighton, a leisure town made spectacularly fashionable by the patronage of King George IV.

The fourth point to bear in mind, and one particularly and poignantly relevant to the protests of rural workers, is that urban growth in this period did not result from wholesale migration from countryside to town the moment the spinning mills of Lancashire began to turn out cotton undergarments. The wildly misleading image of a rural peasantry, 'proletarianised' and dispossessed by the parliamentary enclosure movement between 1760 and 1820 and rushing to the new towns in consequence, should be expunged from our textbooks for ever.

Long-distance migration from countryside to town was very much the exception, relating only to the growth of London, which remained by a huge margin Britain's biggest city (and with a population of 1.7 million in 1831 accounting for one-eighth of England's inhabitants) despite more obvious developments further north; and to emigration from Ireland, which was well underway before the potato famine of 1845–47. The main reason for the enormously rapid growth of the Glasgows, Manchesters and Boltons was short-distance migration from surrounding country-side and, more important still, a high rate of natural increase in these towns because of the extremely high birth-rate. In the rural south, with few alternative job opportunities away from agriculture, population continued obstinately and redundantly to rise until the 1850s, bringing desperation and misery in its wake.

The social context of Britain's early Industrial Revolution is, therefore, complex but important for an understanding of the political struggles after 1815. One point, however, is crystal clear. The economic power base of the country was shifting dramatically and with every year that passed the case for increasing the political representation of the urban and industrial counties from Warwick-shire northwards became more difficult to resist. Yet political change is rarely effected in consequence of genteel, rational calculation and debate; grievance and distress are the more usual stimuli. Neither was in short supply in the hectic years which followed Wellington's victory at Waterloo.

Part Two: Post-War Britain: Crisis 1815–20

3 Lord Liverpool, his Ministry and its Parliamentary Opponents

At the time of the battle of Waterloo, Lord Liverpool's Tory government seemed securely established. Indeed, the victories in the Spanish Peninsula in 1813–14 and the collapse of Napoleon's armies in eastern and central Europe after the Russian campaign of 1812 were themselves factors which helped to stabilise the British government. By 1815 Liverpool had about eighty more regular supporters than his Whig opponents led by Earl Grey and Lord Grenville and this advantage increased somewhat over the next five years (**4**).

Even a secure government in the early nineteenth century, however, could not guarantee an overall majority in the House of Commons, for two reasons. First, in contrast to the situation in the twentieth century, a substantial, though dwindling, minority of MPs were independent of party and saw their duty as representing their constituents in a disinterested manner. Second, among those who were usually disposed to support the government no regular system of 'whips' existed and such support was given on an *ad hoc* or conditional basis. It has been argued by leading authorities that party allegiance in the Liverpool period was not strong and may even have been weakening (**5, 9, 81**). Recent research by the History of Parliament Trust has demonstrated the fallibility of this view (**15**), but spasmodic attendance at debates and the lack of tight party control made the calculation of majorities an uncertain business.

The ability of the Commons to act independently of government policy was most embarrassingly demonstrated in March 1816 when, to reduce the crippling burden of debt run up during the war, the administration proposed to retain income tax, though at a lower rate. Income tax was the most efficient way of raising money from the reasonably well-off that had yet been devised, but MPs needed no reminding that it had been first introduced by Pitt the Younger in 1799 only as a wartime expedient [**doc. 2**]. Opponents of income tax argued that its continuance in peacetime was both an infringement of individual liberties and a breach of faith given the circumstances in which it had first been levied. The City of London presented a petition against the tax which contained 22,000 signatures of merchants, bankers and shopkeepers (**6**).

The government's parliamentary managers had anticipated a comfortable majority, yet they lost the income tax by thirty-seven votes. Viscount Castlereagh shamefacedly reported to the Prince Regent that several had voted against 'whose support had been calculated upon' and it is significant that twice as many MPs representing county constituencies, generally regarded before 1832 as among the more independent-minded members, voted against the government as for it. *The Times* spoke for most property owners when it pronounced in the wake of the defeat that the Commons 'felt with the feelings of the country' (**9**). Thoroughly discomfited, the government immediately agreed not to renew the malt tax, another substantial revenue provider. These two taxes would have brought in £17.5 million in a year, about a quarter of the government's anticipated revenue. The Chancellor of the Exchequer, Nicholas Vansittart, was forced instead to raise money by loans, which pleased the London bankers but stored up longer-term trouble (**4, 55**).

With greater debating talent at his disposal in the House of Commons, Liverpool's taxation policy might have survived. However, as Norman Gash has pointed out, Liverpool was one of nine cabinet ministers in the House of Lords. Of the four who sat in the Commons, only Castlereagh was even a passably effective speaker. Vansittart was poor, and Bragge-Bathurst and Wellesley-Pole (Wellington's brother), patronage appointments hidden away in minor offices, disastrous (**5**). Liverpool's government was by no means unusual in having both more and abler cabinet ministers in the Lords. Especially before 1832, government was controlled by the great landowners of the country, many of whom had inherited their titles and the political influence which went with them. However, in the seventeenth century the Commons had won control over financial matters. A government concerned overwhelmingly between 1815 and 1820 with economic crises, and the political discontents to which they gave rise, should have been more strongly represented in the lower house.

Matters were improved somewhat when the Earl of Buckinghamshire died in 1816 and George Canning took his place as President of the Board of Control. Canning was one of the best speakers in the Commons but his very debating virtues made him an unpopular colleague. His quickness and self-confidence were allied to a waspish wit which was not invariably directed at political opponents. Canning was the source of much ill-feeling in an increasingly cantankerous Cabinet throughout the rest of Liverpool's long ministry. A less controversial promotion in 1818 brought another effective recruit in Frederick Robinson, who was to be one of the main instigators of government economic policy in the 1820s (Chapter 10).

Much the most celebrated recruit to Liverpool's government sat in the Lords. The Duke of Wellington returned home from France at the end of 1818 after duty as both British ambassador there and as supreme commander of the allied army of occupation (**28**). After some reluctance, and an insistence to Liverpool that he was not a 'party man', he accepted an appropriately military cabinet office as Master General of the Ordnance. In 1818, Liverpool felt that Wellington's immense prestige would add necessary weight to a government beset with problems. There is no reason to think that it was in danger of collapse, but Wellington's presence provided reassurance to independent country gentlemen and waverers that Liverpool's was a ministry to be trusted in difficult times. Wellington's acceptance of office inaugurated the second, lengthier and far less distinguished course of his career which saw him as a cabinet minister in various Tory administrations between 1818 and 1846, one of which he led, and which established him very clearly and at times controversially as a 'party man'.

Liverpool's was a thoroughly and uncompromisingly 'Tory' administration in its opposition to 'French principles' of representative government, based on the rights of citizenship; in its defence of property as the essential guarantor of stability; in its belief that if order and unrestrained liberty were in conflict then the former must take precedence over the latter; in its zealous, if not intolerant, defence of the privileges of the Church of England, and its belief that attacks on the church were *ipso facto* attacks on the state; and in its conviction that landed property should be pre-eminent over commercial or moneyed interests. Though a large majority of MPs of all persuasions were landowners, the Whigs had in their ranks roughly twice as many MPs from commercial or urban backgrounds as had the Tories. The Tories had an equivalently dominant representation among retired army or navy officers. Events during the wars had enabled the Tory party

9

profitably to stress its patriotic, as well as its ideological, credentials.

Liverpool's government also emphasised, though it rarely practised, deference to the monarchy. This Liverpool was wont to contrast with the Whig tradition of leadership controlled by the greatest and bluest-blooded of aristocratic families. These families claimed the right to speak for propertied Englishmen, against the interests or prerogatives of the Crown if necessary. Tory commitment was symbolised by Liverpool. Though himself an earl, his father, Charles Jenkinson, had earned his advancement from relatively humble origins by efficient and unswervingly loyal service to George III which had been rewarded with a peerage. Two of Liverpool's most reactionary ministers, Viscount Sidmouth at the Home Office and Lord Eldon, his Lord Chancellor, were – at least in the rarified world of aristocratic politics – *parvenus* from the professional and trading classes. Sidmouth's father had been personal physician to the Earl of Chatham. Eldon, whose reputation during twenty years as Lord Chancellor was one of opposition to virtually every legal reform which was proposed, was the son of a prosperous Newcastle coal merchant. Viscount Castlereagh came from a landed background, but it was an Irish one, and he came to the attention of British politicians as the Chief Secretary who cleaned up the mess left by the Irish rebellion of 1798.

The leaders of the Whig opposition were more homogeneously aristocratic but they could rarely mount an effective challenge to Liverpool. Since they had not anticipated his defeat over income tax, they were not properly prepared to exploit its consequences. More important, however, were divisions within the opposition. The bulk of the 150 or so who voted regularly and consistently against the government were inheritors of the tradition of eighteenth-century Whiggery, held together by the patronage and pull of the great landed families (**12**). They saw themselves as the solid, responsible ballast of the country, supremely equipped alike by their breeding and their broad education to keep it safe from the dangerous, antagonistic extremes of autocracy and republicanism. They believed that the so-called 'Glorious Revolution' of 1688 represented the ultimate triumph of propertied moderation and compromise and saw themselves as inheritors of the tradition of limited monarchy established then. This tradition encompassed support for liberty and, especially, toleration for Roman Catholics and Dissenters.

More recently, the Whig tradition had been diverted (perverted, conservative Whig critics who followed Pitt in 1794 believed) by support for parliamentary reform as the best guarantor of continued broadly-based consent for aristocratic government and by scepticism about, or downright hostility towards, the wars with France. This was the legacy of Charles James Fox, who had died in 1806. His mantle had fallen upon Earl Grey, who as a young radical Whig in the 1790s had been instrumental in persuading Fox to support parliamentary reform.

The titular leader of the Whigs, however, came from a different tradition. Lord Grenville had been a leading minister in Pitt's governments in the 1790s, but had refused to serve Addington because of the new Prime Minister's peace policy after 1801. Grenville had led the brief 'Talents' ministry and, after its dismissal, retained leadership of the opposition (**25**). Grenville was increasingly uncomfortable leading the Whigs after 1815, firstly because he believed in retrenchment and cheap government even more than the Prime Minister and thus ran into conflict with many of the Whigs' more radical allies, and secondly because he was totally hostile to parliamentary reform. In 1817, he finally ceased to work with Grey and other prominent Whigs such as Holland, Lansdowne, Whitbread and Brougham after announcing his support for the government's policies designed to secure law and property against extra-parliamentary agitation (Chapter 4). Parliamentary reform was becoming an increasing embarrassment to mainstream Whigs and in 1816 Holland declared roundly: 'The nearer I look to parliamentary reform the less I own I like it' (**10**). Yet its supporters could not be left in the lurch by the opposition and the Whigs would have to carry their reform cross on into the 1820s, though without the Grenvillites.

Whig performances in the Commons could, on occasion, be very effective. The Whigs had fine debaters, led by men like Samuel Romilly and Henry Brougham, and they could make the more halting Tories look foolish. Increasingly, however, their energies were channelled into specific-issue campaigns, like educational and legal reform, which brought few party rewards. The Whigs were also afflicted by the consequences of personal tragedy. Both Whitbread (in 1815) and Romilly (in 1818) committed suicide and their departure made the prospect of effective collaboration between mainstream Whigs and radical politicians of more democratic temper like Sir Francis Burdett and the irascible Brougham less likely. For many reasons, therefore, the Whigs rarely punched their full weight and they offered Liverpool a less serious challenge than their strength of numbers in the Commons might suggest. As time went on, and helped by fears about extra-parliamentary agitation and disturbance, the Tories under Liverpool became much the more cohesive party.

4 The Revival of Radical Politics, 1815–17

The leading historian of the English working class has called the years which immediately followed Waterloo 'the heroic age of popular Radicalism' (**48**, p. 603). Individual heroisms there were a-plenty. Many leading radicals served terms of imprisonment for opposition to the government in these years; some were convicted of treason and executed. The 'heroic age' implies much more than this, however. Between 1815 and 1820, the government faced a challenge, not only to its specific policies, but to its very authority, which was broader in its base and more significant in its long-term implications than any of those confronting its predecessors.

This is not to say that Liverpool's government was more vulnerable to overthrow than those which went before. Such a claim would be patently absurd. Liverpool, after all, survived when Harold in 1066, Richard III in 1485 and Charles I in 1649 did not. The true significance of the years 1815–20 is that they witnessed increasingly confident attacks on the notion that government should be directed and controlled by a small number of wealthy, and mostly unelected, folk. Legitimate government, it was contended, concerned *representation* rather than inheritance. The principle itself was far from new. It had been raised by numerous radical sects during the 'English Revolution' of the 1640s and 1650s. In Europe, it was the common political discourse of the eighteenth-century Enlightenment. This discourse, popularised and widely disseminated by Thomas Paine and his followers in the 1790s, had challenged the authority of William Pitt during the French Wars, when it had provoked a remarkably solid alliance of property owners against the pretensions of skilled workers and a few writers and intellectuals (**40, 48, 68, 72**).

After 1815, however, that patriotic alliance broke up. In the last years of the war, cotton manufacturers in Lancashire felt the pinch as the economic warfare between Britain and the French destroyed many of their markets. Depression and bankruptcy tested their loyalty to the old order beyond breaking point.

Their workers, laid-off when the mills lost orders, forced to pay

13

high indirect taxes on basic items of consumption like bread, sugar, soap, tea and malt to pay for the war, and hit in 1812 by wheat prices which rose to the stratospheric level of 126*s* (£6.30) a quarter (against a late eighteenth-century average of around 50*s* (£2.50) (**4**, p. 402), were susceptible to the reformist arguments of the veteran radical John Cartwright as he toured the industrial districts of the midlands and northern England in that year and again in 1813 and 1815. By the end of the war, parts of England which had either ignored or been lukewarm towards parliamentary reform in the 1790s were now not only receptive but beginning to generate their own leaders and their own political consciousness.

Liverpool's government after 1815, therefore, faced dual challenges which threatened to coalesce in a mighty engine of agitation which a landowners' Parliament would be powerless to resist. On the one hand, it was losing the support of the manufacturing interest, particularly in the north of England. On the other, working people, whose disaffection had previously been concentrated in places like London, Norwich and Sheffield – older urban centres occupied by literate and politically-aware skilled men – were showing an increasing tendency to challenge the government in the new industrial centres of Manchester, Stockport, Bolton and Leeds (**35, 48**). The Industrial Revolution was making its first serious impact on the political life of the nation.

In this context, Lord Liverpool's decision in 1815 to introduce a new protective tariff against the importation of foreign corn was particularly significant. Corn laws were not new. As recently as 1804 a law had been enacted imposing punitive duties on the import of corn when the domestic price fell below 63*s* (£3.15) a quarter (**55**), p. 6). The 1815 corn law prohibited the importation of any foreign corn until domestic prices reached 80*s* (£4). Its political impact was dramatic. Liverpool soberly told the House of Lords [**doc.1**] that the purpose of the new law was to guarantee continued domestic production at a time of falling prices. This would not only stave off famine – a constant government worry at a time of population growth – but also help to stabilise prices.

Outside Parliament, and particularly in the urban areas of the country, an entirely different interpretation was put on Liverpool's motives. *The London Chronicle* pointed out that 'the landed interest want to have a law for raising the price of corn to double the amount of what it was before the war began' (**46**, p. 190). Henry Hunt, rapidly making a name for himself as an effective platform orator with an instinct for the political jugular, wrote a pamphlet in which he insisted that though a landowner himself, the only interpretation that could be put upon the bill was that it was for 'the benefit and aggrandizement of a few rapacious landholders ... at the cruel expense of the hitherto greatly oppressed community' (**65**, pp. 48–9).

The 'greatly oppressed community' had direct ways of showing its displeasure. The passage of the 1815 corn law was attended by riots in London during which troops had to defend Parliament. Elsewhere, the political temperature was raised several notches. Unproductive landowners were depicted in entrenched positions against productive workers. This was to prove the more important response since it changed the focus of disturbance. Rioting was endemic in eighteenth-century society and, when it had a political rather than an economic basis, its motivation was likely to be conservative if not atavistic. The anti-Catholic Gordon riots of 1780 and the anti-Dissenting and anti-reformist Priestley riots of 1791 are prime examples.

By the early nineteenth century, however, the legitimacy of laws passed by unrepresentative Parliaments was being challenged. The new corn law was seen as the work of landowners who thought only of their own pockets. No amount of argument by Liverpool in the Lords or Vansittart in the Commons could convince the inhabitants of northern industrial towns otherwise. The corn law concentrated minds on the issue of parliamentary reform as the only effective means of redress. It is hardly surprising that the reform movement in this period was so anti-aristocratic. At the same time, pro-establishment rioting and crowd activity all but disappeared.

The great political catalyst of the period was economic distress. With the coming of peace, the government no longer needed armaments or so many uniforms. It was also forced into deflationary policies by the defeat of its taxation proposals (see above pp. 7–8) while the demobilisation of about 400,000 servicemen glutted an already depressed labour market. Wages in 1815–16 were squeezed downwards, especially in rural areas where unemployment was most acute and the cost of relieving the poor was highest. By 1817 poor law relief, which had cost rate-payers only £2 million in the mid-1770s, had reached almost £8 million. In East Anglia, agricultural labourers, long considered inert and entirely unpolitical, rioted, burning ricks and demanding bread. Slogans such as 'Bread or Blood' circulated widely and figures associated with authority, such as harsh poor law overseers or grasping

15

parsons and clerical magistrates, were singled out for abuse and attack (**39, 41, 88**).

The evidence of Samuel Bamford, a leading Lancashire radical working man and admittedly no impartial witness, nevertheless indicates the geographical extent of discontent in 1815 and 1816:

'At Bridport, there were riots on account of the high price of bread; at Bideford there were similar disturbances to prevent the exportation of grain; at Bury, by the unemployed, to destroy machinery; at Ely, not suppressed without bloodshed; at Newcastle-on-Tyne, by colliers and others; at Glasgow, where blood was shed; at Preston, by unemployed weavers; at Nottingham, by Luddites, who destroyed thirty frames; at Merthyr Tydville on a reduction of wages; at Birmingham, by the unemployed; and at Dundee, where, owing to the high price of meal, upwards of one hundred shops were plundered'. [**doc. 16**]

In such a disturbed climate, the cause of parliamentary reform revived. Whereas in the 1790s, it was uncertain whether the leadership of this cause was in the hands of aristocratic Whigs or extra-parliamentary artisan radicals, after 1815 no doubt remained. Radicalism focused on a reform of Parliament and that focus lay outside Parliament itself.

Following the lead given by Major John Cartwright, numerous Hampden Clubs (taking their name aptly from John Hampden who opposed arbitrary government in the form of Charles I's ship money in the 1630s) were formed in the last years of the war and immediately afterwards. All of them called for reform but many, especially in the Lancashire cotton towns, went against Cartwright's more modest proposals and called for a government elected by full manhood suffrage.

In this, they were encouraged by the emergence of a much more self-confident radical press. It is difficult to exaggerate the importance of radical newspapers both as an educative and a cultural force. Journals like William Cobbett's *Weekly Political Register*, T. J. Wooler's *Black Dwarf*, William Hone's *Reformists' Register* and Thomas Sherwin's *Political Register* were read aloud and discussed at meetings in public houses known to be sympathetic to radical or democratic causes, thus spanning the gulf between the literate and the non-literate. All but the first of these were founded in the years immediately after the war.

Printing the editorials of his *Register*, first launched in 1802 but selling at a prohibitively expensive one shilling (5p), on a single sheet ironically called *Twopenny Trash*, enabled William Cobbett, a journalist of genius, to reach a mass audience. From November 1816, circulation spiralled. At a time when 5,000 was considered an excellent sale for a national newspaper, Cobbett claimed 'sixty or seventy thousand' for his cheap *Register*. For this mass audience he had both a direct and an indirect message. Firstly, he asserted plainly to his readers that 'misgovernment' was the cause of their distress. His target, therefore, was what he called 'Old Corruption', that patronage system of appointments controlled in their own interest by an unelected landed elite. Secondly, he worked on the self-regard of his readers. Addressing 'Friends and Fellow Countrymen' in November 1816, he plainly told them that 'Whatever the Pride of rank, or riches or of scholarship may have induced some men to believe . . . the real strength and all the resources of a country, ever have sprung and ever must spring, from the *labour* of its people' (**48**, pp. 620–21) [**doc. 17**]. Never one to underestimate his own influence, Cobbett claimed that the effects of his work were 'prodigious; the people everywhere on the stir in the cause of parliamentary reform' (**69**, p. 385).

Radical clubs and political newspapers were two means of advancing the democratic cause. The third, and most alarming one to the government, was the monster demonstration backed by mass petitions to Parliament for redress of grievances and acknowledgement of rights. The presentation of petitions was a long-established, and perfectly constitutional practice, of course, but the campaigns of 1816–17 injected a coercive element. The strategy developed by the demagogic utterances of Henry Hunt at the three meetings held in Spa Fields, London, was to show the authorities the force of public opinion and its latent power if petitions for reform were denied. The largest such meeting was held in December 1816. It passed resolutions calling for annually elected Parliaments and universal suffrage. Provincial meetings were also held. One such, at Thrushgrove on the outskirts of Glasgow in October 1816, was reported to have been attended by 40,000 people. In Sheffield in December a splinter group broke off from the main reform demonstration, and carried a blood-stained loaf – symbolizing 'Bread or Blood' – around the town. Some windows were smashed and the leader of the group was arrested (**46**, pp. 207–8).

In January 1817, at Cartwright's instigation, a meeting of delegates from radical societies throughout the country met at the

Crown and Anchor tavern in London. In the manner of many such radical gatherings between the 1790s and the 1840s, there was much disagreement over tactics and much opportunity for radical spokesmen to demonstrate that their commitment to reform was at least equalled by their commitment to self-advertisement and aggrandisement. The radical MPs for Westminster, Francis Burdett and Lord Cochrane, were both alienated by Hunt's determination immediately to present a petition for annual Parliaments and universal suffrage. The reformers' case was not so strongly represented in Parliament that the radicals could afford to alienate sympathy there and, outside Parliament, both Cartwright and Cobbett had severe disagreements with Hunt and the mainly northern delegates who supported him.

As in the 1790s, reformers divided into camps which might be broadly distinguished as 'constitutionalist' (those who would proceed only by argument and rational persuasion), and 'coercionist' (those who either advocated violent overthrow of the existing constitution or, like Hunt himself, were prepared to use the threat of violence to put pressure on the authorities). As in the 1790s, also, it suited the government's book to believe that the radical cause had been hijacked by violent revolutionaries. Like Pitt, Liverpool set up a 'Committee of Secrecy' which heard much evidence, some of it accurate, some of it the exaggeration or pure fabrication of spies and *agents provocateurs*, of revolutionary preparations [**doc. 21**].

The main blame was laid on the followers of Thomas Spence, a Newcastle bookseller who had died in 1814, but who had converted many to his plan for radical reform based upon the expropriation of private estates and the nationalisation of land. These 'Spencean Philanthropists', who included Thomas Evans, James Watson, Arthur Thistlewood and Thomas Preston, made no secret of their republicanism and some of them were engaged in revolutionary preparations late in 1816. Watson and Thistlewood were alleged to be involved in looting gunsmiths' shops and attempting an attack on the Tower after the December Spa Fields Meeting [**docs. 19 and 20**]. They were tried for high treason but acquitted later in 1817. The Committee of Secrecy had 'no doubt . . . that a traitorous conspiracy has been formed in the metropolis for the purpose of overthrowing, by means of a general insurrection, the established government, laws and constitution of this kingdom, and of effecting a general plunder and division of property'.

The government's legislative response also bore an uncanny resemblance to Pitt's in 1795. In February and March 1817, habeas corpus was temporarily suspended, allowing suspected persons to be held indefinitely without charges being brought against them. A new Seditious Meetings Act prevented societies and clubs holding meetings without the approval of magistrates. Sidmouth, the Home Secretary, sent out circulars to magistrates reminding them of the wide powers they had to suppress disturbance, and urging their use when needed. As in the 1790s, also, the measures had at least temporary success. Reform meetings became far less frequent. William Cobbett hastily left the country for the United States, though not before angrily denouncing an offer of £10,000 allegedly made to him by Sidmouth on condition that he stopped publication of the *Register* and retired to his Hampshire farm (**69**, p. 391).

The government was probably not as alarmed about revolutionary preparations as it liked to pretend. Its spies kept it very well informed; a good intelligence system and pre-emptive force against that minority prepared to challenge its new legislation proved sufficient. Despite the arduous endeavours of some historians both to unearth conspiracy and lionise the conspirators, the evidence points more to the desperation of hunger than to careful, concerted revolutionary planning. Samuel Bamford and other well-informed radicals tried to dissuade handloom weavers gathered in Manchester in March 1817 from marching to London to present a petition to the Prince Regent. About 300 of the 4,000 who had assembled ignored the advice and set out with blankets strapped to their backs for bedding – hence the grandiose title 'The March of the Blanketeers'. They got no further than Stockport, seven miles away, where they were turned back by the local yeomanry. A brief scuffle ensued in which one man was killed.

Plots for a more general rising in the spring of 1817, hatched mainly in those areas of Yorkshire and the east midlands where there had been Luddite disturbances five years earlier, were expertly infiltrated by a government agent known as 'Oliver the Spy', in reality a discharged debtor, W. J. Richards. The planned 'rising' became in June a sad, doomed march on Nottingham by about 200 men led from the Derbyshire Peak District of Pentrich by Jeremiah Brandreth, a skilled worker in his late twenties. Forty-five men were arrested and charged with high treason. Three, including Brandreth, were executed and the majority of the rest joined the ever-swelling number of politically undesirable convicts in the new colonies of Australia.

On one level, the events of the first half of 1817 were a major success for the government. Public reaction to its vigorous response, however, was far from uniformly favourable. The radical press was much more effective than its establishment counterparts and it continued its campaign of vilification, arguing – with some Whig support – that the government had misjudged the public mood and had over-reacted. With characteristic restraint, the editor of *Gorgon*, John Wade, accused the government of 'the most abominable practices recorded in history' (**48**, p. 663). Liverpool's ministers were soon to discover that, with no war to rally the loyalty of propertied opinion, and with an ever more self-conscious and self-confident industrial sector of the economy unsympathetic to Tory politics, reform would be far less easily controlled after 1817 than in the 1790s.

5 Peterloo and the Cato Street Conspiracy

After the March of the Blanketeers, the government enjoyed a brief respite from radical activity. The 1817 harvest was good. Trade revived in Lancashire where literate and politically-aware weavers had been giving much strength to radical protest since 1812. Unemployment fell. In consequence, 'hunger politics' were less apparent. The government remained chronically short of cash but its position at Westminster was strengthened by the defection of the Grenvillites from the Whigs in 1817 (see above, p. 11). It could trust the political nation with a general election in 1818 from which it emerged, as in the previous election of 1812, with more than twice as many seats as the Whigs and a slightly strengthened position overall (**15**, i, pp. 235, 263). The repeal of the Seditious Meetings Act and the reinstatement of the Habeas Corpus Amendment Act in 1818 were tangible evidence of declining alarm.

Some political protest continued in 1818, of course. The radical press still published vigorous condemnations of government policy. Wooler's *Black Dwarf* took over from the *Political Register* as the leading organ of protest during William Cobbett's sojourn in the United States [**doc. 22**]. The *Manchester Observer* began publication in January 1818 and advocated immediate parliamentary reform. Its circulation between 1818 and 1821 was substantial, although its impact was regional and short-term. Political clubs still met in public houses. Parliamentary reform petitions bombarded Westminster. It has been estimated that 1,500 were received in the course of 1818 (**46**, p. 211).

The improvement of trade brought a revival of trade union activity with the Lancashire weavers much to the fore. Trade unions, or 'combinations' as they were called, were all formally banned between 1799 and 1824 but, thinly disguised as sickness and benefit insurance clubs, they continued to exist. Between 1812 and 1814 textile weavers' unions had led campaigns against reduced wages and against the introduction of unskilled workers into their trade, thus 'diluting' it. They had also sought, unavailingly, to preserve apprenticeship as a necessary condition of entry

21

to trades. Both power-loom and handloom weavers sought wage increases during the spring and summer of 1818. Their strategy was to use a period of good trade, and thus relative labour scarcity, to coerce employers into diverting some of their profits into weavers' pockets. Radical political societies supported the weavers' claims and, after one demonstration in 1818, the Stockport yeomanry, which included manufacturers, shopkeepers and a few conservative skilled workers, used force to disperse rioters. It was to prove an unhappy precedent.

The failure of the weavers' agitation, combined with a worsening economic climate from the late summer of 1818, led to renewed concentration on politics and the formation of a 'Union for the Promotion of Human Happiness'. This union, which provided a lead for many others in the north of England in 1818–19, was organised on the basis of co-operation between skilled workers and the lower middle classes. Its objective was parliamentary reform. The unions emphasised the close links between radical politics and religious nonconformity, and they also placed an emphasis on education. If working men were to vote, they must know the issues upon which their choices would turn. Many Sunday schools now became political as well as religious agencies – much to the annoyance of evangelicals who had supported the Sunday schools of the late eighteenth century as bastions of order and conservatism, where young minds could be trained up to industry, virtue and a dutiful acceptance of the existing social hierarchy.

The participation of women in radical politics was also a feature of these years. Some separate 'Female Unions' were formed early in 1819, apparently more alarming to the authorities than were their male counterparts. Stockport women reformers were accused of 'demoralizing the rising generation' and training 'their infants to the hatred of every thing that is orderly and decent, and to rear up rebels against God and State' (**35**, p. 232).

With the return of want to the industrial north, radical leaders were once again able to organise mass meetings. In January 1819, Henry Hunt addressed a large crowd at St Peter's Fields, Manchester, and urged them to ignore Parliament and present a petition directly to the Prince Regent demanding universal suffrage and annually elected Parliaments. Meetings in Birmingham and Leeds elected delegates from towns currently unrepresented in Parliament who were to meet in London and consider further action. Such meetings could be interpreted as a direct challenge to the authority of Parliament. Reports from spies and *agents provocateurs* reached the

Home Secretary, Sidmouth, claiming that arming and drilling were taking place among radical groups.

Fears of a breakdown of public order, which some constructed as preparation for rebellion, were therefore rife when Hunt accepted an invitation to address yet another open-air meeting in Manchester in August 1819, organised by the Patriotic Union Society. Hunt's appeal for a peaceable assembly cut little ice with Lancashire magistrates who had seen previous meetings end in violence and who knew that the political temperature in the summer of 1819 was higher than ever. When upwards of 60,000 men, women and children assembled in St Peter's Fields on 16 August, the local authorities were determined not to let the meeting take its course. On Home Office advice, Hunt was arrested but the rest of the day's events owed nothing to central government. The meeting was forcibly broken up by the yeomanry and, when they got into difficulties, by hussars using sabres. More than 400 people were injured in the dispersal and eleven either sabred or trampled to death. The event was speedily dubbed 'The Peterloo Massacre' in a bitingly ironic reference to Wellington's most famous victory.

Peterloo provided the radical cause with martyrs and the press exploited the situation to maximum effect. Liverpool's government felt obliged to defend the Manchester and Salford authorities but the defence had a hollow ring, as the Prime Minister himself privately admitted. In the growing public clamour for reform, the Whigs were forced to take up the question again. Their enthusiasm was warmed when the government dismissed Earl Fitzwilliam from his post as Lord Lieutenant of Yorkshire for supporting Hunt's meeting. Nothing rallied Whig opinion so effectively as a Tory humiliation of one of the great landowning families, and Fitzwilliam was a mainstay of Whig support in the north of England.

Peterloo also made reform into a national cause. Political unions were formed in areas of the country, such as Newcastle-on-Tyne and the Black Country area of south Staffordshire, where radicalism had previously been weak. By the autumn of 1819, even the formation of 'armed associations' of property owners could not quieten the reformers, and threats of violence increased. Rioting was commonplace and the rumours of arming and drilling intensified. Liverpool's old colleague, Lord Grenville (see above p. 11), urged him to pass stern legislation to stave off a British revolution on the French model.

For the last time during the pre-1832 period, the government responded to the call for reform with repression. The Six Acts (or 'Gagging Acts' as they were not inappropriately dubbed) were rushed through Parliament in December 1819. These Acts prohibited any gatherings for arming or drilling; gave magistrates in the disturbed areas powers to search for arms; prevented defendants from gaining delays by postponing their answers to specific charges; prohibited meetings of more than fifty persons without magistrates' consent, and indemnified magistrates against the consequences of casualties suffered in dispersing illegal assemblies; increased the penalties for writing seditious or blasphemous libels; and imposed punitive stamp duties on pamphlets and papers which had been fomenting discontent. The Acts were a commentary on recent disturbances and, by regulating both meetings and the press, indicated clearly enough where the Tories laid the blame.

The Acts were used selectively to remove radicals from the scene. Hunt, Wooler, Richard Carlile and even the aristocratic radical MP Sir Francis Burdett were all locked up by the summer of 1820. The efficiency of Sidmouth and his intelligence-gathering activities perhaps deserve greater emphasis than they have received. Historians out of sympathy with the Liverpool government, as most in recent years have been, lay articulate and sympathetic stress on the extent of radical activity. Yet it was contained. The crisis of 1819 was met decisively but the government avoided unselective brutality. The situation was one which could easily have been mishandled by a Tory government and, left to the prejudices of Eldon, a Lord Chancellor of little political sensitivity, it would have been. The firmness of Liverpool and Sidmouth has earned them little approbation but political judgements are more often made on the basis of utilitarian than philosophical criteria. It is not necessary to sympathise with the government's objectives to appreciate its competence in a crisis. As E. P. Thompson remarked on Pitt's similar policies in the 1790s, the government's bark proved much worse than its bite. Political acumen was needed to understand that a loud bark was what the government guard-dog needed. Wholesale biting might indeed have led to shooting the dog.

In 1819, as in 1795 and 1817, legislative action proved sufficient to contain the radical challenge. In reality this challenge was less concerted and less effectively led than might appear from the noise it made and the alarm it induced in some quarters. Very different views about tactics and even ultimate ends were held by radical sympathisers. It was one thing to accept that the unreformed House of Commons was increasingly at variance with early nine-teenth-century British society, quite another to agree on a specific reform programme. The preponderant weight of radical opinion between 1815 and 1820 was indeed democratic, but influential middle-class reformers, like old John Cartwright, continued to favour a household suffrage. Parliamentary Whig reformers tended to be even more cautious, preferring to disfranchise rotten boroughs, give seats to leading industrial towns and soberly debate what qualification for the vote best fitted an emerging industrial age. Such a gradualist approach invited the contempt of radical populists such as Hunt, Cobbett or Carlile.

Disagreements on means were even more debilitating. Richard Carlile was a disciple of Tom Paine who extended Paine's repub-lican sentiments into an almost pathological hatred for the Church of England as an agency of conservatism and mystification. His reaction to the Peterloo Massacre was unequivocal: 'The People have now no recourse left but to arm themselves, immediately, for the recovery of their rights' (**66**, p. 34). Democratic radicals divided broadly into 'moral force' and 'physical force' camps. Moral force leaders, among whom were many nonconformists and trade union-ists, continued to believe, as Paine had done, that the concentrated power of reason trained on the ramparts of hereditary privilege and vested interest would bring about a peaceful transition of power. Physical force leaders, citing Peterloo, drew the less sanguine conclusion that vested interest cannot be argued into renouncing its privileges. Force must be met with force. Many advocates of physical force, however, of whom Henry Hunt was the pre-eminent example, were prepared to threaten violence in order to coerce while being reluctant to put their threats into practice.

It might be argued that hungry handloom weavers and factory operatives were badly let down by their leaders in 1819–20. Hunt and Cobbett, certainly, had self-regarding, vainglorious streaks which got in the way of realistic planning. Too many radical leaders were windbags, carried away by their rhetoric and heedless of the effects their intoxicating language had on empty stomachs and unprepared minds. More important, however, was the evanescence of radicalism. Though Peterloo had excited massive national hostility, radicalism remained largely concentrated in London and the textile districts. Its mass appeal was critically determined by bread prices and unemployment levels.

Liverpool and Sidmouth were also shrewd enough to realise that every threat of violence alienated middle-class support. The middle classes had no particular love for Liverpool's protectionist agricultural policies which, indirectly, threatened industrial markets, but fear for their property was a much more potent factor in 1819. It should be remembered that representatives of an alarmed Lancashire bourgeoisie cut swathes through the reform crowds in St Peter's Fields. Even in the autumn of 1819, the threat of revolution was not so great as radical activity made it seem and the best hope of constitutional reform, which lay in alliance between the middle and working classes against the landowners, was actually reduced by the alarm which reports of arming and drilling generated. The Six Acts were welcomed by the bourgeoisie, and those with little or no property to lose had insufficient unity of purpose and decisive leadership to compensate.

Genuine revolutionaries are not deterred by adverse legislation and a few of these existed both in England and Scotland in 1819–20. The Spencean (see p. 18) Arthur Thistlewood was already familiar to the authorities by 1820. He had instigated the riots which followed the London Spa Fields meeting in November 1816 and had embarrassed the authorities several times since then. For one such, a challenge to Sidmouth for a duel, he had been imprisoned without trial for over a year in 1818–19. On his release, which coincided with Peterloo, he began to lay revolutionary plans in London with a fellow Spencean, Dr James Watson, and members of the recently formed London 'Committee of Two Hundred' (**48**). Rumours began to circulate that Thistlewood and Watson were planning a nationwide rebellion with the help of revolutionaries in Lancashire and Yorkshire. A simultaneous rising early in 1820 was planned to coincide with the assassination of the entire cabinet as they attended a dinner at the house of Lord Harrowby. As usual, the conspiracy was infiltrated by a government agent, in this case George Edwards. The authorities were able to apprehend the conspirators as they assembled in Cato Street in February. Thistlewood and four accomplices were speedily tried for high treason and executed three months later. Five others were transported.

Sidmouth, not given to hasty or alarmist utterances, nevertheless believed the Cato Street conspiracy to have been part of a wider plot. The theory is supported by a number of outbreaks both in Scotland and Yorkshire immediately after the conspiracy's failure was apparent. An attempt by weavers to seize Glasgow predictably failed but about twenty men decamped to Bonnymuir in Stirling-shire, led by Andrew Hardie and John Baird. There they offered battle to the yeomanry and hussars who came in search of them. A similar number from Strathaven, under the leadership of a veteran radical from the 1790s, marched to Glasgow at the same time but fled when the hopelessness of their position became clear, as it rapidly did. These three leaders suffered the same fate as Thistlewood, while the lesser lights were transported (**72**, pp. 73–81). Within a week, Yorkshire weavers had attempted to take control of Huddersfield. More than three hundred assembled on the moors outside Barnsley carrying flags and weapons. John Blackwell, a journeyman tailor who had organised a post-Peterloo reform meeting in Sheffield, tried to seize the Attercliffe barracks in that city (**46**).

The doomed and desperate efforts of the spring of 1820 deserve mention not because they offered any real threat to the government – though it is worth noting that assassination attempts only need to succeed once – but because each drew on a much broader base of pro-reform sympathy. London, industrial Lancashire, south and west Yorkshire and central Scotland were all substantially disturbed in late 1819 and early 1820. The government was well-positioned to anticipate trouble from revolutionaries but it did not make the mistake of assuming that only small bands of desperadoes were disenchanted. One of its rising stars, Robert Peel, perhaps put it best in a private letter to a fellow Tory, John Wilson Croker:

'Do not you think that the tone of England – of that great compound of folly, weakness, prejudice, wrong feeling, right feeling, obstinacy and newspaper paragraphs, which is called public opinion – is more liberal, to use an odious but intelligible phrase, than the policy of the government?' (**20**, p. 250–1).

No one could mistake Peel for a political reformer, but by the middle of 1820 some anti-reformers were beginning to consider how best 'respectable opinion' might be assuaged and whether recent events had given greater credence to hotheads and revolutionaries. Peel, for one, did not believe that the reform question would disappear with the return of prosperity.

6 The Curious Affair of Queen Caroline

Only against a background of disturbance does the tragi-comedy of the Queen Caroline affair make sense. Yet in 1820–21 it severely embarrassed Lord Liverpool, lost him the confidence of George IV, and almost brought about his dismissal from office. The affair also gave rise to the last great wave of public demonstrations before the Reform crisis.

The background details are quickly told. Prince George had married his cousin Princess Caroline of Brunswick-Wolfenbuttle in 1795, an earlier marriage to Maria Fitzherbert in 1785 having been quietly ignored. The new union was never a close one and both partners quickly sought alternative outlets for their not inconsiderable energies. Once Regent, and freed from his father's claustrophobic orthodoxy on the subject, George hastened to put his unloved wife to one side. She was bribed with a yearly annuity to leave the country in 1814, moving to Italy where she soon settled to an existence of insouciant promiscuity. Some of the more salacious details were revealed to the Regent in 1819 in a report which he intended to make the grounds of a divorce action. Other than via her yearly *douceur* of £3,000, Caroline had no contact with the Regent. She was not even informed of the death of their only child, Princess Charlotte, in childbirth in 1817 – an event of some dynastic significance since it left George with no direct heir.

George III died on 29 January 1820 and George IV wasted no time in informing his ministers that, outweighing all other considerations of state, his urgent priority was a divorce. Caroline's name was not to appear in the Anglican prayer book; Caroline was not to be crowned as his Queen. Liverpool and his ministers urged caution. The country was still in a disturbed condition, and such action against the Queen would provoke national hostility which, given the inevitable delays attending any contested divorce, would be indefinitely prolonged.

Much turned on the new King's personal unpopularity. The Hanoverians had not inspired much affection since they had saved the nation for Protestantism in the unedifying shape of George I in 1714. The fourth George, however, plumbed new depths, embodying all the worst failings of his dynasty: inflexibility; petulance; fierce, unpredictable and uncontrollable rages; promiscuity; and an incorrigible lack of political sense. George's own numerous sexual indiscretions had received wide, and mocking, publicity. During the recent disturbances the Regent's personal habits had been lampooned by radical cartoonists. Their representation of George as a fat, flatulent, dissolute slob, indeed, served as an allegorical indictment of aristocratic government. As Liverpool knew all too well, the King's suing for divorce could only mobilise the nation on behalf of the Queen, whatever her own shortcomings.

Furthermore, the new Queen was determined to play a full part in the unfolding drama. She signified her intention to return to England where she would contest divorce proceedings with vigour, and would accept support from any quarter. In the early months of 1820, indeed, she was relying on the advice of the radical master draper and former Lord Mayor of London, Matthew Wood. He informed her that the people of London would prove stout champions. Thus fortified, Caroline published an open letter in leading newspapers in which she lambasted her husband for his despicable actions and for using his influence to close all European courts to her. She asserted her constitutional rights as the King's wife and proclaimed, 'England is my real home to which I shall immediately fly' (**6**, p. 90).

In the circumstances, the failure of Liverpool's hastily-devised plan to prevent the Queen's arrival is hardly surprising. He employed Henry Brougham, the prominent Whig lawyer who had maintained contact with Caroline since about 1812, to negotiate with her and to offer her £50,000 if she remained outside Britain (**27**). By the time Brougham, whose concern for his own political career complicated matters, made the offer, the Queen was deaf to financial entreaty, having already committed herself to her English escapade. Her much-publicised arrival in London in June brought huge crowds onto the streets in her support (**45**).

Frustrated in its main objective, the government was forced to do the King's bidding. It introduced a Bill of 'Pains and Penalties' and began a trial of the Queen before the House of Lords on a charge of maintaining 'an adulterous connection with a foreigner'. Between August, when the trial began, and November, when the Bill was ignominiously withdrawn in the face of dangerously dwindling majorities in the Lords, the press had a series of circulation-boosting field days. The King was held up to ridicule as a licentious hypocrite accusing his wife of the very vices he had so long and so assiduously practised. *The Times* took the Queen's part along with the rest. William Cobbett, who could see no other issue in the autumn of 1820, acted as the Queen's unofficial adviser and filled his *Political Register* with passionate articles in her defence (**45**). Cartoonists of genius, like George Cruikshank and William Hone, depicted the King of England in ever more ridiculous, degrading and humiliating postures. Never has the British monarchy been held in greater contempt.

Tumultuous crowds thronged the capital at Queen Caroline's every appearance; the city was illuminated in triumph on the day the Bill was withdrawn (**46**). The Caroline affair is often described as an episode in London radicalism, but it was in fact a national event. The Whigs organised county protest meetings against the Bill in Yorkshire, Northumberland, Durham, Buckinghamshire and Sussex (**12**). Newcastle-under-Lyme, in Staffordshire, was only one of many towns to send petitions in favour of the Queen. More than half the adult male population signed it. A congratulatory address followed when the Bill was withdrawn.

So soon after the Peterloo furore, the government could well have done without a further *cause célèbre*, especially one which it had tried hard to avoid. His peevishness reinforced by his mauling, the King blamed his troubles on his ministers. Had the Whigs not been split, as ever, on whether they would make a measure of parliamentary reform a condition of accepting office, it is probable that the King's bluster would for once have been translated into decisive action. The Whigs might well have come into office in December 1820 [**doc. 3**].

The affair did produce one ministerial casualty whom Liverpool could ill-afford to lose. George Canning, though increasingly frustrated by what he considered junior office as President of the Board of Control, and ostentatiously aware that his talents exceeded those of most of his colleagues, was the government's most incisive debater in the Commons. His relationship with Caroline had been close, and some informed gossip suggested that it exceeded the bounds of propriety. Canning opposed the prosecution of the Queen, absented himself on a convenient European tour during its course, and eventually sent his resignation to the Prime Minister in December 1820. At the time, it seemed a devastating blow.

The arrival of Christmas afforded a breathing space during which propertied Englishmen could reflect. The Caroline affair was of no more permanent significance in the political constellation than the appearance of a comet. It dazzled its watchers while it lit up the late summer and autumn skies, but it was only a squalid squabble between a couple of coarse, graceless and obstinate, though highly privileged, individuals. This marital strife, whatever its publicity value, was not worthy of a ministerial crisis. Nor, as more reflective or high-minded radical writers like Wade and Wooler came to conclude, did the affair afford a proper springboard from which to launch a new reform campaign. So, while country gentlemen continued to conclude, as they had at least since 1816, that the Tories were a sounder bet than the Whigs, radicals outside Parliament continued their quest for a higher plane of political argument and a more elevated cause with which to mobilise the masses.

In any case, as the new year dawned the redundantly vindicated Queen had nowhere to go. She would not be divorced but neither would she be permitted to exercise the duties of a Queen. When she accepted a pension of £50,000, she lost whatever residual support she had for a renewal of the constitutional battle. The King would not let her attend his coronation in July 1821. Yet Caroline demonstrated her lack of judgement by turning up uninvited at Westminster Abbey and banging on every door in turn in a vain attempt at admittance. As many in the large, and still sympathetic, London crowd must have realised, it was a characteristically public, yet futile, gesture.

The end, however, was near. Caroline, presumably weakened by the strident exertions of the past year, succumbed with unexpected speed and decisiveness to a fever in August 1821. The King rejoiced. The Prime Minister, a naturally more magnanimous and reflective figure, could afford genuine condolence. His government had already drawn strength from falling prices and a return of prosperity (Chapter 8). The Whigs' dream of office had evaporated. Even before her final illness, Caroline had become a political irrelevance. The London crowds forced a diversion of her funeral *cortège* through the City from the planned anonymity of its route to Harwich and thence to a final resting place in Brunswick, but this proved to be the last even vaguely menacing public assembly of the lower orders which Liverpool's government would have to face, although it would survive for another five and a half years. The comet had burned itself out.

7 Foreign Policy under Viscount Castlereagh

British foreign policy between the battle of Waterloo and the first Reform Act needs to be placed in the context of reaction to the major war which had disrupted Europe in the previous twenty years. As in the still greater world-wide conflagrations which ended in 1918 and 1945, the efforts of the victorious powers were bent towards creating conditions which would preserve the peace for future generations. As 1918 brought the creation of the League of Nations and the last months of the Second World War the United Nations, so the allies which had combined to defeat Napoleon created something called 'Congress Diplomacy'. This derived from an agreement, made by Britain, Austria, Prussia and Russia at the Congress of Vienna in 1815, to meet at regular intervals to monitor the workings of the peace settlement they had agreed to impose upon defeated France and also to discuss matters of mutual concern (**4**, p. 414).

This Congress System was a major achievement of Viscount Castlereagh, Britain's foreign secretary from 1812 to 1822. Castlereagh was acknowledged by contemporaries to have been the prime mover of a settlement which would preserve the peace of Europe for forty years. This was a major achievement in itself and especially in the light of the fact that eighteenth-century Europe had witnessed much warfare between the major powers even before the outbreak of the French wars in 1792.

The new 'system' associated Britain much more closely with peacetime diplomacy in Europe than had traditionally been the case. In a sense, this was inevitable. Britain had been the one constant adversary of the French since 1793 and had emerged from the wars with an enhanced reputation as a great power. Looked at from the Austrian or Prussian viewpoint, no European settlement without Britain's assent after 1815 would look secure or permanent.

The break with tradition, however, attracted criticism. In 1814–15 many argued that the French, as a defeated nation whose revolutionary ideology, no less than its recently all-conquering armies, had wreaked such havoc in Europe, should be made to pay a much heavier price than Castlereagh thought it wise to exact. Once the Congress System was in place, Castlereagh's enthusiastic diplomacy was attacked in Britain as the delusion of a man whose head had been turned by hob-nobbing with the great figures of Europe like Tsar Alexander I of Russia or the Austrian foreign minister, Prince Klemens Metternich. Britain's interests, it was urged, would be better served by detachment from minor squabbles between European emperors and autocrats [**doc. 10**] The country should rather follow those world-wide interests to which island status, maritime heritage and commercial considerations all seemed to point.

Castlereagh's diplomacy, however, was perfectly consistent. He had no greater desire than his critics to see Britain engaged in further European warfare, but he saw interventionist diplomacy as the best means to ensure this objective. Seeing Austria, Prussia and Russia – the other three powers who, with Britain, signed the Treaty of Chaumont in 1814 to defeat France – all as potential disturbers of the European balance by becoming themselves too powerful, Castlereagh sought to hold each in check. In pursuit of this objective he could see much merit in preserving the territorial integrity of smaller powers on which any of the other three might have designs (**62**). His determination to offer France peace with honour derived from the hard-headed assumption that the humiliation of one of Europe's leading powers was no recipe for the long-term stability which Britain needed to pursue its commercial and colonial interests both in Europe and further afield.

Taken as a piece, Castlereagh's 'Congress strategy' owed much to the ideas of his old mentor, the Younger Pitt. When trying to stitch together a coalition against Napoleon in January 1805, Pitt suggested to the Russian ambassador that the eventual restoration of peace must be accompanied by 'a general Agreement and Guarantee for the mutual security and protection of the different Powers and for re-establishing a general System of Public Law in Europe' (**61**, p. 95).

Castlereagh's influence at the peace settlement was immense. The very presence of a British foreign secretary at a European conference table was unusual and Castlereagh capitalised upon it, winning golden opinions even from practised and devious diplomats for his hard work, his ability to gain the respect of the protagonists and his straightforwardness. He did not obtain all that he wanted, of course. A plan to strengthen Prussia, which he wished to see as a source of stability in northern-central Europe, by negotiating its take-over of neighbouring Saxony, came to nothing. Nor was he able to secure Poland from effective Russian control. These two reverses assumed greater significance later as it became clear that the main threat to Britain's European interests in the nineteenth century was to be Russia rather than France.

Nevertheless, on all the most crucial immediate issues for Britain, Castlereagh got his way. The sprawling empire of nepotism which Napoleon had created was dismantled. Yet, though France was forced to accept an army of occupation under the Duke of Wellington until 1818, all attempts to cut into her pre-1789 territories were blocked. Louis XVIII, younger brother of the executed Louis XVI, was confirmed after a long exile in Verona as the lawful Bourbon King of France, though he ruled within certain constitutional constraints. The Austrian Netherlands and Holland, however, were merged into a single kingdom as an effective buffer against French northward expansion. Castlereagh, recalling the campaigns of Louis XIV in the 1670s, was convinced that it was France's fixed ambition 'to possess herself of the Low Countries and the territories on the left bank of the Rhine' (**61**, p. 101).

The reorganisation of Germany into a confederation of only thirty-nine states also afforded prospects of greater stability, particularly since Prussia gained substantial territory in the Rhineland, including a crucial border with north-eastern France. Castlereagh hoped to see Prussia develop as the north German counterbalance to the Austrian Habsburg Empire in the south. The Spanish monarchy was restored in the unprepossessing person of Ferdinand VII in 1814 while Italy, always an area of potential unrest in view of its numerous states, was substantially reorganised. The Habsburg Empire took over the economically prosperous northern states of Lombardy and Venetia, while Savoy and Genoa were annexed to Piedmont-Sardinia. The Papal States were restored and Naples saw the return of a Bourbon monarch. As a result of these adjustments, the respective spheres of monarchical influence were more sharply defined.

Castlereagh was not foolish enough to demand mainland European territory as the price of British victory over the French, though Hanover, whose Elector was still the reigning British monarch, gained some. Britain's commercial and strategic influence, however, was substantially enhanced by the settlement. The island territories captured during the wars were retained. The most important of these were in the West Indies where Britain kept control of St Lucia, Tobago and Trinidad. Guyana, on the north-eastern tip of South America, was taken from the Dutch. In Europe, the North Sea island of Heligoland was acquired from Denmark, while Malta soon became Britain's guard dog in the Mediterranean. The Ionian Islands, off the west coast of Greece, also became British in 1815. The world-wide extent of Britain's interests was symbolised by the acquisition of the Cape of Good Hope, Ceylon, Mauritius and the Seychelles. Opportunities for British traders in the east were substantially increased by these acquisitions. Singapore was added in 1819, breaking the Dutch trading monopolies in the East Indies.

With French and Spanish influence substantially reduced in the West Indies and the long-standing Dutch pre-eminence in the Far East at an end, Britain's supremacy as a world-wide trading nation was by 1820 unchallengeable. The foundation stones of what one historian has called 'Britain's Imperial Century' (**63**) were laid during and immediately after the French Wars, long before her major African territorial acquisitions in the 1880s and 1890s.

Castlereagh's direct concerns, however, rarely strayed outside Europe. From the earliest days of the peace settlement, important differences of interpretation separated Britain from her allies. Put simply, Britain sought a balance of interests in Europe to prevent any one nation from becoming threateningly powerful. Forms of government were of secondary importance. Despite much contemporary criticism, in which the poet Byron was prominent, Castlereagh did not believe that the ideological forces of liberalism and nationalism which had been let loose during the eighteenth-century Enlightenment and the French Wars, either could or should be suppressed. No Irish politician in the nineteenth century – Castlereagh was an Ulsterman from the so-called 'Protestant Ascendancy' – could be unaware of the importance of nationalism. Since Britain already had a representative government of sorts, its politicians were less fearful of deviations from the autocratic norm than were most hereditary rulers.

It was not surprising that the European emperors saw the settlement of 1814–15 as a means of confirming the supremacy of the old order. In September 1815, Tsar Alexander I persuaded the Emperor of Austria and the King of Prussia to agree to 'remain united by the bonds of a true and indissoluble fraternity' and to 'lend each other aid and assistance' when required. It rapidly became clear that Alexander intended this 'Holy Alliance', as it soon became known, to be the means whereby nationalist or liberal movements in any part of Europe could be crushed. Britain had refused to sign the Holy Alliance and soon needed to defend its own, very different, interpretation of 'Congress diplomacy'.

At only the first Congress held under the arrangements made in Vienna – that of Aix-la-Chapelle in 1818 – was there anything approaching unity among the great powers. Here arrangements were completed for re-admitting France, now an apparently secure monarchy, into the small circle of the great powers. The Quadruple Alliance became the Quintuple Alliance and France agreed 'to concur in the maintenance and consolidation of a System which has given Peace to Europe'.

Even at Aix-la-Chapelle, however, differences had surfaced about how the system should develop. Tsar Alexander was making aggressive noises against nationalist forces threatening Spanish territories in Latin America, but his plans for collective action to force the nationalists to back down came to nothing. However, between 1818 and 1821 liberal and nationalist movements in Europe, which affected Spain, Portugal and Naples, brought the ideological issue to the forefront. When the Greeks rebelled against the Ottoman Turks in March 1821, demanding independence, all the major European powers were affected, either by considerations of strategy or sentiment or both. Greece, of course, was the cradle of European civilisation and most English statesmen knew considerably more Greek literature than they did contemporary science or economics.

At the Congress of Troppau in 1820, called by Alexander to discuss recent events in Spain, Portugal and Naples, the powers agreed on a 'Protocol' which would refuse recognition to any regime established by rebellion and which reserved the right to 'exercise effective and beneficial action' to restore 'legitimate' government to countries where rebellions had been successful (**61**, p. 105). Significantly, Britain was not a party to this Protocol. Indeed, Castlereagh had refused to send a full representative to Troppau. His observations on the conduct of the members of the Holy Alliance were set out in a famous State Paper written in May 1820 [**doc. 11**].

Study of this important document should indicate not only Castlereagh's level-headed pragmatism but how little of substance separated him from British critics of his foreign policy. Castlereagh was no heedless interventionist and he saw dangers in extending the principles of Vienna into a reactionary coalition. More than most conservative European statesmen, he understood that the ideas released by the French revolution would not be suppressed by force of arms and he was not prepared to see broader considerations of strategy sacrificed on the altar of dogma. The reference to 'the spirit of Treason and Disaffection' in Britain is particularly significant in this context.

As early as 1820, therefore, different interpretations of the European 'system' presaged its downfall. The Congress adjourned at Troppau re-convened at Laibach at the beginning of 1821. British support for action against liberals and nationalists was severely limited. Castlereagh briefed his brother, Lord Stewart, who represented the government, on the important distinction to be drawn between intervention on principle and intervention where a great power's 'immediate security, or essential interests are seriously endangered by the internal transactions of another state' (**18**, p. 208). Such an interpretation would justify Austrian intervention to suppress nationalism in Naples, since Austria was a major power in Italy, but it could not justify Tsar Alexander's sending troops to Spain or Portugal, because no direct Russian interest could conceivably be at risk. The distinction was also pragmatically convenient, since Britain's relations with Austria were much warmer than those with Russia; in addition, with the advent of the Greek rebellion, the interests of the two nations were in close accord and opposed to Russia.

Castlereagh wryly noted that the principles which Tsar Alexander fiercely upheld in Spain and the Americas could be conveniently bent when Russian interests were at stake. The Greek rebellion offered an opportunity for Russia to establish itself in the eastern Mediterranean at the expense of the Turks; few were fooled by the assertion that Russia wished to intervene to support rebellious, but Christian, nationalists against 'legitimate', but infidel, Turkish authority. British trading interests were directly affected by events in the Mediterranean and Castlereagh would not permit Russian initiatives in this area to go without challenge.

The Laibach Congress agreed to defer consideration of these weighty matters and it was decided to hold a fresh Congress at Verona in October 1822. By the end of the Laibach meeting, however, it was clear that the respective, and increasingly conflicting, interests of the great powers were assuming much greater importance than were abstract declarations of conservative principle. To that extent, events proved Castlereagh's instincts sound.

By the summer of 1822, however, Castlereagh himself was far from sound. The Duke of Wellington wrote despairingly in early August that Castlereagh, whose 'sober mind' had previously been his hallmark, was now 'in a state bordering upon Insanity' (**28**, p. 38). Perhaps depressed by the overwork generated in combining conduct of foreign policy with domestic duties as Leader of the House of Commons, certainly alarmed by the prospect of a public accusation of homosexuality (for which allegation, incidentally, there is very little evidence), the Foreign Secretary cut his throat on 12 August, dying almost immediately. His death provoked a ministerial crisis but, as we shall see (Chapter 12), it did not produce dramatic shifts in the substance of British foreign policy. The collapse of Congress Diplomacy, and Britain's renunciation of close European accords, for which Canning is usually given the credit, had been not only anticipated but accepted by his predecessor.

Part Three: Post-War Britain: Stability 1821–27

8 The Return of Prosperity

'Never in our memory was this part of the country in a state equally flourishing: our manufacturers are employed, our artisans happy and industrious, and loyalty and content have given place to jacobinism and sedition, which distress had mainly contributed to foster' (**35**, p. 254).

The *Stockport Advertiser* was reflecting in June 1823 on the buoyancy of the cotton trade rather than on the economy as a whole. Nevertheless, it has been generally accepted that for most of the 1820s the economy was flourishing. After the dislocations of the immediate post-war period, which were accompanied by high levels of unemployment and high food prices, trade revived and distress ebbed.

As the *Stockport Advertiser* also implied, trade revival reduced the levels of working-class discontent. Mass protest movements were very rare between the end of the Queen Caroline affair and the end of Liverpool's government in 1827. Radical leaders locked away in 1819–20 were generally released in 1821 and 1822. The most charismatic of them, Henry Hunt, was let out of Ilchester gaol in October 1822 (whence, typically, he had launched a series of stinging, if self-absorbed, diatribes on the state of British prisons). His release was joyously celebrated in many places but these celebrations were by a small number of convinced political radicals; they did not occasion mass agitation or the threatening postures of 1819–20 (**65**).

For much of the 1820s, radical energies were absorbed in longer-term strategy and ideology. As ever with the reform movement, squabbles broke out, most notably between Richard Carlile, who wished to see radicalism follow both a republican and an atheistic course [**doc. 23**] and Hunt, who knew how few radicals were atheists and how strong had become the links between reform and nonconformity. In this decade both Thomas Hodgskin, a journalist who had served as a naval officer during the Napoleonic Wars, and

William Thompson, an Irish landowner converted to the utopian socialism of Robert Owen, advanced theories which stressed labour as the source of all value, and which had obvious implications for later socialist movements (**48, 56**). Developments in these years contributed to the maturity of later protests but they did not immediately threaten the government.

Prosperity was the keynote of the 1820s, but it was neither universal nor continuous. Remarkably little is known about key indicators such as unemployment, for which no official records were kept until the 1890s. Thus, historians are reliant on impressionistic contemporary accounts of the 'state of trade'. National statistics which do survive are far less sophisticated than those available in our own day and they anyway assume the existence of a *national* economy which, even in the early stages of the Industrial Revolution, is highly dubious. Movements within different sectors of the economy often contrast markedly and regional differences may be much more significant than national trends. Nevertheless, some obvious statements may be made with confidence. The economy grew much more rapidly in the 1820s than in the 1810s. The gross national product is estimated to have fallen by 3.5 per cent in the 1810s before rising by 16.8 per cent in the 1820s. All the conventional indicators used by economists to demonstrate growth are firmly in place. Capital formation, stock-building and total investment all show growth figures in the 1820s well ahead of those in the 1810s. Overall investment seems almost to have doubled in the 1820s (**52**, i, p. 131; **doc. 7**). However, while manufactures, mining, building, trade and transport grew at an overall rate of about 26 per cent in the 1820s, agriculture, having declined sharply as food prices plummeted at the end of the French wars, increased by only 4.6 per cent (**51**, p. 166).

Agriculture remained depressed from the end of the French wars until prices began to pick up in the middle of the 1830s. Only the presence of the Corn Laws (see above, p. 14) prevented even greater falls. Landowners and tenants, especially corn growers, who had invested heavily and, as it turned out, unwisely when prices were high and credit cheap in the 1790s and 1800s, were put under severe pressure during the allegedly 'prosperous' 1820s, as the pages of the frequent parliamentary committees on agricultural distress made woefully clear. It is worth noting that a 'landowners' Parliament' tolerated the fact that the agricultural sector of the economy fared much worse than any other in the decades before the first Reform Act. The irony was not lost on many backbenchers, concerned that the government was too sympathetic to the needs of commerce and to the theories of a new generation of political economists who preached free trade as the surest route to prosperity (**4, 55; docs. 4** and **6**). Agricultural labourers, whose numbers continued to increase while job opportunities dwindled, did worst of all. Even the normal means of relief, the Poor Law, became more stringently administered and more difficult to obtain during the 1820s (**37**). Protests by rural labourers, in the form of rick-burning and attacks on Poor Law overseers, were common in East Anglia, especially in 1822 (**33**).

For townsfolk, the main factors in the prosperity of the 1820s were the general buoyancy of economic activity which increased employment opportunities, and the fall in food prices. A long-running and, on the whole, not very enlightening argument has raged on the implications of industrial growth for the living standards of working people between about 1780 and 1850 (**4, 38, 47, 52, 84, 85**). The main facets of that debate do not concern us here, but it is worth noting that both 'optimists' and 'pessimists' agree that during the 1820s real wages (which are calculated by comparing movements in money wages with those of prices) rose. This was largely because the cost of bread, still the staple diet of most British people, fell sharply. The average price of wheat (from which most bread was made) was more than one-third lower in the 1820s than in the 1810s. Even in the peak price year of 1825, wheat at 68*s* 6*d* (£3.42) a quarter was 25 per cent lower than the average price for the 1810s (**4**, p. 402). The very cause of agricultural distress, therefore, was the main factor in increased prosperity elsewhere [**doc. 5**].

In addition to agricultural labourers, the other large group of workers whose living standards almost certainly fell in the 1820s was the weavers. Handloom weavers were the most obvious casualties of technological advance. Their numbers had expanded rapidly in the late eighteenth century when the process of spinning was mechanised before weaving. This situation had created a substantial but short-term demand for weavers, whose wages during the French Wars had risen substantially. From the 1820s, however, the introduction of the new power loom reduced their earning power and in the most industrialised areas of the country first their wages and then their numbers began to drop sharply. In Stockport, for example, 5,000 handloom workers were employed in 1818. Over the next four years, the number declined to less than 3,000 and by 1832 to about 800 (**35**, p. 255). In London's East

End, the Spitalfields silk weavers, whose numbers had likewise grown in the early years of the century, endured both wage cuts and unemployment from the mid-1820s partly as a result of the reduction of protection and a growing market for imported manufactured silks (**70**).

During the years of prosperity, therefore, while most social groups benefited, more from lower prices than from higher wages, those who were threatened by the quickening pace of technological change faced crisis. The long-term outlook was also bleak for skilled workers whose bargaining power was threatened by competition from the unskilled who worked long hours in 'sweat shops' or 'slop shops' where products of inferior quality were made for a developing mass market. Tailors and shoemakers in London, for example, long considered among the aristocrats of labour, found it ever more difficult to maintain wage differentials. Rapid population growth, of course, increased labour supply (Chapter 2). In most periods of economic boom, higher general levels of prosperity disproportionately benefit the better-off. Although living standards almost certainly rose for most people in the 1820s, therefore, the gap widened between the middle classes, whose income came mainly from profit and investment, and the working classes, dependent more or less exclusively on wages.

It is characteristic of rapidly industrialising societies that their economic progress, remarkable overall, is subject to short-term fluctuations. Even during the boom of the 1820s, one sharp slump was experienced, caused by excessive speculation in the money markets. The banking crisis of 1825–26 involved the failure of thirty-six country banks and more than sixty substantial London finance houses (**53**). The government only narrowly avoided having to instruct the Bank of England to suspend payments to creditors in cash, which would have had a disastrous effect on investors' confidence. The crisis precipitated major banking reforms (Chapter 10). In the real world of labour and employment, the crisis had important effects. Unemployment temporarily rose in the cotton and woollen districts of Lancashire and Yorkshire and among the building and other skilled trades of London. Some rioting and machine breaking was experienced in the spring and summer of 1826. At Chadderton, near Manchester, in April, indeed, seven rioters were killed by troops during attacks on mills which had introduced the new power looms (**46**, p. 233). The prosperity of the 1820s stood on brittle foundations.

9 'Liberal Toryism' and the Achievement of Lord Liverpool

'Liberal Toryism' is the description often given to the second, and shorter, period of Liverpool's administration. It is said to date from the major ministerial changes made between August 1822 and January 1823. In this brief period, which begins with Castlereagh's suicide, six of the thirteen portfolio cabinet posts changed hands: Canning took over the Foreign Office, and his old position of President of the Board of Control (with special responsibility for Indian affairs) went first to Bragge-Bathurst and then to Grenville's friend Charles Wynn. The old Chancellor of the Exchequer, Nicholas Vansittart (ennobled as Baron Bexley), became Chancellor of the Duchy of Lancaster, and was succeeded by Frederick Robinson. Robinson's successor as President of the Board of Trade, and thus responsible for commercial policy, was William Huskisson. Viscount Sidmouth, indelibly associated as Home Secretary with the Peterloo Crisis and the 'Six Acts' (Chapter 5), was in his mid-sixties by 1822 and quite keen to retire. He remained in the Cabinet for two more years largely because the King wished it, but only as Minister without Portfolio. His postponed retirement nevertheless turned out to be a very lengthy one since he died in his late eighties in 1844. Sidmouth's successor at the Home Office was Sir Robert Peel, not yet in his mid-thirties, but with substantial ministerial experience in Ireland behind him; more recently he had been chairman of an important parliamentary committee on financial management (Chapter 10). He was widely regarded as the ablest politician of his generation. Of the major ministers, only Liverpool himself and Wellington retained their old posts.

These reshuffles have been seen as marking a genuine transition in Liverpool's government from a 'reactionary' phase, associated with popular unrest and its suppression, to a 'liberal' one associated with a wide range of reforms in domestic and commercial affairs and a new stance in diplomacy. The impression is reinforced by an influential monograph on the 1820s entitled *Lord Liverpool and Liberal Toryism* (**8**). Nevertheless, the term is misleading and should be used only with great caution. Certainly, Liberal Toryism should not imply a conscious conversion from one policy to another. Liverpool's notion of Toryism has been indicated above (pp. 9–10) and he embraced it no less warmly in 1827 than in 1815. It also incorporated from the very beginning a strong preference, implanted by Pitt, for free trade. The trade liberalisation of the 1820s (Chapter 10) was not a new policy.

Circumstances mainly, and personalities to a lesser degree, determined that the last five years of Liverpool's government would be more concerned with commerce than with public order and with cautious experiment rather than with fearful retrenchment. Liberal Toryism was not, however, a new brand of reforming Toryism; its ideological basis reflected the influence of the Younger Pitt. There are close parallels between Pitt's peacetime policies of 1784–93 and Liverpool's between 1822 and 1827. Similarities also exist between Pitt's stress on public order between 1793 and 1801 and Liverpool's between 1815 and 1820.

Liverpool lacked the independence and intellectual vision to strike out in new directions. He was a consolidator rather than an innovator and he was happy to follow the policy guidelines set out by his great predecessor. This is why Disraeli described him a little later as the 'arch-mediocrity'. Certainly, his fussy, detail-ridden caution could infuriate bright subordinates, notably George Canning. Such character traits do not necessarily make for ineffective government, however, particularly when they are combined, as in Liverpool's case, with shrewd judgement about colleagues and a willingness to let able and trusted subordinates get on with the job.

The Prime Minister also recognised a duty to 'bring on' young men. He could also see political advantages in having able politicians like Peel and Huskisson carrying the burden of debate against the Whigs in the Commons. These men, however, had all served loyally in junior posts in the 1810s and did not regard their promotion as an opportunity to change government philosophy. As we shall see (Chapter 10 and 11), much of the groundwork for the reforms, adjustments and improvements of the 1820s had been put in train both by their allegedly 'reactionary' predecessors and by themselves as subordinates. The real distinction is not philosophical but practical. Huskisson and Peel proved more effective both in debate and in administration than their predecessors.

For three main reasons, therefore, the term Liberal Toryism

should be used with care. Firstly, it did not imply any kind of government 'conversion' in 1822. Secondly, the new men were only 'new' in seniority within the government and, for the most part, developed policy guidelines agreed before they achieved cabinet rank. Thirdly, the 'liberalism' (itself an ambiguous word) of the 1820s was more 'improving' than reformist and operated against a background of prosperity rather than, as for most of the period 1815–21, economic crisis. None of Liverpool's cabinet was more persuaded of the desirability of thoroughgoing parliamentary reform in 1824, say, than in 1815. The Whig leader Lord John Russell introduced a Bill in 1822 to disfranchise a hundred of the smallest, and most corrupt, parliamentary boroughs. The seats thus released would have been redistributed to larger industrial and commercial towns and to the bigger counties. The Bill received no government encouragement and failed by a large majority in the Commons (**4**, p. 376).

The idea of enacting reform because of extra-parliamentary pressure remained anathema. It is tempting to see the route to the passage of the Great Reform Act in 1832 in linear terms: a Tory government, fearful of reform, cracks down in the 1810s, then becomes 'liberalised' during the prosperity of the 1820s. Liberalisation makes the reforming task of the Whigs much easier when they finally achieve office in 1830. This simple model, cherished by many students, is wholly wrong. Such Tory 'liberalisation' as there was remained firmly within the old, closed political world. No sympathy was shown for the franchise demands of middle-class and working-class radicals outside Parliament. Not until the Toryism which Liverpool knew and nurtured was shattered after his death (Chapter 13) did parliamentary reform become a practical possibility.

Although the ministerial changes of 1822–23 did not signal any changes of principle, they did have a political purpose. The Caroline affair (Chapter 6) and the antipathy towards his ministers which it had produced in George IV had weakened Liverpool's government. Vansittart's inadequacies showed up embarrassingly when the government was on the defensive and Sidmouth had lost what little command he had in the Commons in the aftermath of Peterloo. The Whigs were able to win some minor, but cumulatively significant, victories in the Commons by obtaining backbench support. In March 1822 they carried a motion to cut the navy estimates and consider reductions in taxation to landowners hit hard by the fall in agricultural prices (Chapter 8). Only threats of resignation by Liverpool pulled independent but Tory-inclined backbenchers back into line and it was clear that new faces on the government front bench were sorely needed.

The long process of estrangement between the Grenvillites and the Whigs (p. 11) was now concluded by Liverpool's determination to strengthen his ministry. The Grenvillites' new leader, the Marquis of Buckingham, had his loyalty to the government cemented by a dukedom and Charles Wynn obtained minor Cabinet office. Of greater long-term significance was the appointment of Marquis Wellesley (Wellington's brother) as Viceroy of Ireland. Like most of the Grenvillites, Wellesley favoured Catholic emancipation and his appointment worried Liverpool's many anti-Catholic supporters. It served its immediate purpose, however. Whig hopes of bringing Liverpool's government down had probably been pitched too high even during the Caroline affair and they took a knock with the Queen's death in 1821. Bereft already of some of their ablest figures (Chapter 3), the Whigs lost heart when the ministerial reshuffle tilted the political arithmetic still further against them. Grey indulged in one of his periodic withdrawals from active political involvement and party discipline slackened from 1823 onwards (**12**). The Whigs after 1822 were rarely able to raise more than a hundred supporters in any parliamentary division. The party battle in Parliament was less keenly fought in the mid-1820s than at any time since 1815.

The hiatus in party rivalry, however, was accompanied by growing divisions within the Cabinet. The knowledge that one's parliamentary position is secure often encourages independent, if not insubordinate, lines of action and the reshuffled government proved much more fractious than its predecessor. Wellington, Westmorland and Eldon all had doubts about British commercial policy both at home and abroad. These surfaced from time to time, notably in the winter of 1824–25 when the King criticised what he called the unwise 'Liberalism' of his government (**19**, p. 233). More serious was the growing split between the 'Protestants' and 'Catholics'. The Protestants comprised the group above plus Peel; they opposed any political concessions to Catholics, expecially in Ireland. In this they had the full support of George IV. The 'Catholics' were led by Canning, as ambitious as he was tactless, and beginning to anticipate parliamentary life after Liverpool. Their group, which included Huskisson and the old Grenvillites, favoured giving Catholics both the right to vote in parliamentary elections and to sit in Parliament.

Liverpool had tried to keep Catholic emancipation on the political back-burner. The issue had ended the younger Pitt's ministry in 1801 when George III had dug in his anti-Catholic heels with that obstinacy for which he was famous, and Liverpool knew what passions it still aroused in the country. He also considered it the only issue on which George IV could not be budged, bribed or cajoled. The emergence of Daniel O'Connell's pro-emancipation and anti-Union Catholic Association raised the political temperature in Ireland after 1823 and frustrated Liverpool's hopes. Only a strong 'Protestant' majority in the House of Lords prevented both a measure of emancipation and government salaries for Irish Catholic clergy being accepted in the spring of 1825, following a campaign led by the radical MP Francis Burdett in the Commons. Both Liverpool and Peel came close to resignation. The Catholic question was the major issue in the general election of 1826 and it brought Tory disagreements firmly into the public eye for the first time since the end of the French Wars.

In the months before February 1827, when Liverpool suffered the cerebral haemorrhage which caused his resignation, therefore, his government was as divided as at any time in the previous fifteen years. To the contentious issues of commerce and Catholic emancipation was added in 1826 further disagreement over the right policy for corn (pp. 54–5). A poor harvest in 1825 had brought a sharp rise in wheat prices and the hot summer of 1826 threatened supplies of other foodstuffs. This, against a background of renewed distress in the north of England, caused ministers to scrutinise afresh the policy of protection for domestic corn producers. Huskisson and Wellington disagreed on the issue and the by now customary battle lines within the Cabinet were ready to be drawn again. Unkind critics asserted that Liverpool's concern to balance opposite forces within his government only created an atmosphere of vacillation and weakness. Some even believed that real power had passed to Canning already.

In fact, Liverpool's authority remained unchallenged to the end. He may have lacked vision and originality but he possessed a gift which sustains many balanced, decent and considerate folk – and Liverpool, despite his fussiness, was all three. He inspired trust. That trust he used to his political advantage, since he was able to persuade intrinsically abler colleagues to work under him when they would have been reluctant to accept the authority of anyone else. Where Pitt, who was Prime Minister for even longer, collected acolytes, Liverpool sought only the loyalty and respect of his colleagues. It is doubtful if he even considered himself a leader, although his ability to retain the loyalty of brilliant, but divergent, subordinates in the last years of his Prime Ministership certainly required leadership qualities. In his last years, he used wisely the experience gained through a lifetime in politics.

Why he survived as Prime Minister for so long has perplexed many. Harsh critics have asserted that he survived precisely because survival, rather than leadership, was the height of his ambition. Long tenure of power was anyway easier when general elections were infrequent and most parliamentary seats not actually contested. In such circumstances public opinion, however hostile, was far less important than it was later to become. Before Liverpool, Walpole, Pitt and the formidably mediocre Lord North had all been Prime Minister continuously for more than ten years and all had successfully faced public hostility at least as great as anything encountered by Liverpool. Only looked at in a twentieth-century context does Liverpool's longevity seem remarkable. Liverpool's political world, after all, was destroyed between 1828 and 1832 and survival in the highest office became much more difficult under the new rules.

In a society dominated by property owners who feared change and who had seen the chaotic consequences of ill-considered change in revolutionary and Napoleonic France, a Prime Minister who fully shared those fears and who could keep the lid on the kettle in Britain would retain support sufficient at least to survive from the landowners who dominated Parliament. The 'Six Acts' of 1819 had massive parliamentary support. In addition, Liverpool was fortunate that his uncertain early years as Prime Minister coincided with the years of victory over Napoleon.

These factors help to explain Liverpool's long tenure of power but they do not tell the whole story. They ignore the support on which Liverpool was able to rely in Cabinet. They ignore the immense variety of political experience which Liverpool had acquired before he became Prime Minister in 1812. His unrivalled knowledge of the workings of government and administration he put to great, and constant, use as Prime Minister. He was much more than a mere chairman of Cabinet meetings, as his frequent informed letters to colleagues reveal. They ignore the skill with which he conciliated awkward and prickly ministers, especially after 1822.

Perhaps most of all, they ignore the speed with which Britain was changing and the variety of problems that the pace of change engendered. No 'arch-mediocrity' could have kept abreast of developments and reacted to different circumstances as Liverpool was able to do. So, while Liverpool survived in part because he did not attempt too much, he was shrewd enough to see that he could not proceed, as many of his backbenchers would have preferred, by venturing nothing, merely defending existing interests against the gales of social and industrial change. In appreciating when and by how much to defend existing institutions and when and by how much to seek to change them, he showed considerable tactical skill. Of course, those skills were deployed for a conservative purpose. His aim was to preserve an old order where property (particularly landed property) and hereditary succession determined the distribution of power. More than most of his contemporaries, however, he knew how to apply Edmund Burke's famous dictum that 'A state without the means of some change is without the means of its conservation'. It is important that Liverpool be judged by the criteria of his own time and by what he was attempting to achieve. The true measure of his political abilities is perhaps best demonstrated by the speed with which the Tory party destroyed both itself, and much of the old order it aimed to preserve, once Liverpool's experienced guidance was removed.

10 Trade, Taxation and Finance

For several years after the end of the French Wars, British finances were in a mess. To pay for the wars, Britain had borrowed heavily and the burden of loan repayments distorted government finance. In 1815, government expenditure exceeded income by 45 per cent and almost 80 per cent of that expenditure went on servicing a grotesquely swollen national debt (**4, 5**). Since country gentlemen would not permit the retention of income tax [**doc. 2**], Liverpool embarked on a policy of savage retrenchment and cost-cutting to balance the books. Government expenditure was reduced by 50 per cent between 1815 and 1818, largely because of demobilisations in the armed forces. The sailors and soldiers thus released did not readily find jobs (Chapter 4) and high levels of unemployment contributed substantially to the high cost of poor relief which reached a peak of £7.8 million in 1818. Since rates to finance this relief were being paid by property owners who already complained about excessive taxation, it is not surprising that the government ran the risk of alienating not only the poor, among whom radical politics made substantial headway between 1815 and 1820, but also their own natural constituency.

Matters were not helped by the manifest inadequacy of Nicholas Vansittart as Chancellor of the Exchequer. His main response to debt was to raise new loans, mostly from the City of London, to pay off old debts. This kept interest rates higher than a depressed economy could bear. Landowners, already heavily in debt thanks to wartime investments made on the assumption that agricultural prices would remain high, protested mightily at their mounting debts when they fell.

Government economic policy between 1815 and 1819 was one of drift, in anticipation of some natural process of adjustment to conditions of peace. In 1819, Liverpool, harried by an opposition Whig party growing in confidence after some modest gains in the general election of 1818 and by increasing pressures from back-benchers, was forced to respond. He believed that business confidence would be restored only when the British currency returned to valuation on a gold standard, and when the Bank of England redeemed all notes on demand with gold or coin. Cash payments by the Bank had been suspended by Pitt in the crisis year of 1797. However, Liverpool knew how contentious this change in policy would be and he was not temperamentally inclined to take decisive initiatives on controversial issues.

Nevertheless, he was persuaded to sanction the appointment of two select committees, one to consider the state of the currency and the other to examine public finance generally. These committees became important policy makers. Although the government was strongly represented on both, it would be an exaggeration to say that their deliberations reflected government initiatives. In a sense, Parliament drove Liverpool towards trade regulation.

Peel, who chaired the Currency Committee, rapidly concluded that Britain's system of paper currency fuelled inflation and reduced the value of the pound in foreign markets (**20**, p. 242). The Committee's recommendation of a staged restitution of cash payments represented a victory for the increasingly influential political economists, led by David Ricardo, who argued that permanent prosperity could only be achieved with a sound currency. It was also to the liking of William Huskisson, a protégé of Canning. Huskisson was tucked away in the obscurity of the Department of Woods and Forests before 1823 but his economic influence grew steadily. He believed that peace had brought only stagnation of trade and that productive investment had been discouraged (**55**, p. 31). Country gentlemen generally favoured the resumption of cash payments; the gold standard symbolised plain dealing and represented a rebuff for those City fund holders who had profited from speculation. In fact, the return to the gold standard was completed by 1821, in advance of the Committee's timetable.

The Committee on Finance urged a reduction in the size of the national debt. Vansittart, with some reluctance, responded. His 1819 budget reduced the Sinking Fund and raised £3 million in indirect taxes, including a new duty on malt which increased the price of beer. The objective was a balance of income and expenditure. To Liverpool this represented the long-postponed return to post-war normality. He told Huskisson in September 1820 that only now, with the prospect of a fixed currency and the disappearance of 'annual loans' to bale the government out, was the nation 'settling itself into a state of peace' (**55**, p. 66).

Britain's budgets did indeed mostly balance between 1819 and

1827. The budgeting strategy generally associated with 'Prosperity Robinson' was begun in the last years of Vansittart's stewardship, though 'Old Mouldy' or 'Poor Van', as he was variously known, only followed a policy set by others. Small surpluses and the return of 'normality' persuaded Liverpool that lowering tariff barriers would be the best long-term guarantee of national prosperity. In this, as in much else, he followed Pitt. Government economic policy after 1820 returned to the road down which Pitt had begun to travel during his peacetime administration of the 1780s with its emphasis on commerce and low tariffs. The policy also swam with an ever more powerful intellectual tide. Free trade was urged by political economists like David Ricardo and J. R. McCulloch with all the fervour of a moral crusade.

A famous speech delivered by Liverpool in May 1820 anticipated tariff reductions but carefully avoided specific commitments. The spadework was being done by parliamentary select committees on which government supporters were in a majority. The most influential was the Foreign Trade Committee chaired by Thomas Wallace, one of the unsung but substantial influences in the free trade movement. His Committee recommended in 1820 a relaxation of the Navigation Laws, whose purpose had been the aggressive protection of British shipping, and also a reduction in the charges imposed on foreigners using British warehouses. In 1821 Wallace shepherded first through his Committee and then the Commons a reduction in the differential duty paid on Baltic as against Canadian timber. This modest change has been described as 'the first practical step towards implementation of the principle of *laissez-faire* in the post-war period' (**54**, p. 116), and it was followed by five similar reductions in 1822 designed to extend opportunities for British traders, especially in northern Europe.

Wallace began a process of rationalising and simplifying the complex legislation which weighed down trade with some 2,000 separate statutes. These restricted not only the movement of goods and raw materials but also the emigration of skilled workers and the export of machinery. Such protection for a nation whose industrial output greatly exceeded that of all her competitors made no sense; it merely invited retaliatory tariff walls and a general restriction of trade worldwide. Between 1822 and 1825 first Wallace and then Huskisson reduced the number of monopolies and relaxed the tight restrictions of the Navigation Laws. The most important measure was Huskisson's Reciprocity of Duties Act of 1823. Under it, any nation which agreed to reciprocal reductions could transport goods to Britain on the same terms as British ships. Huskisson's aim was to reduce the cost of imports to British manufacturers. He also wished to resume trading patterns between the USA, Britain and the British West Indian colonies (**55**).

The complement of this policy was the lowering of domestic duties in the annual budget. Robinson's first budget, in 1823, concentrated on direct taxation. The removal of some £2 million was designed to mollify landowners who had suffered from reductions in prices and rents, as soon as the availability of a surplus permitted. The focus of the budgets of 1824 and 1825, however, was on customs and excise duties. Duties on rum, coal, wool and silk were reduced in 1824. In 1825, while the trade boom provided increased government income despite reductions in duty, a thorough revision of the tariff system was begun. Robinson aimed to stimulate domestic demand by lower prices and (like Pitt in the 1780s) to reduce the illegal attractions of smuggling. Duties on a range of manufactured goods were reduced from 50 per cent to 20 per cent and on raw materials from 20 per cent to 10 per cent. The recovery of the British economy was sufficiently strong for the short slump in the winter of 1825–26 to be absorbed. Robinson was able to budget for further government surpluses in 1827. Between 1821 and 1827, despite lower duties, customs revenue increased by 64 per cent (**19, 4**, p. 193).

Such changes did not make Britain a free-trade nation. Modest protection remained, with a trading system now much more efficiently administered. The commercial interests government policy was designed to benefit responded pragmatically. As expounded by men like Ricardo, Wallace and Huskisson, the new economic policy was not always linked to specific interests and markets. Thus, while older trades and businesses saw reductions of duty as a possible threat to established markets, newer ventures tended to respond more enthusiastically to the opportunity to find new markets for their products.

The 1820 petition of London merchants in favour of free trade, sometimes cited as evidence of commercial unanimity, in fact reflected careful, and unrepresentative, lobbying by the political economist Thomas Tooke. Those trading enterprises which had been heavily protected since the seventeenth century were not notably enthusiastic political economists. The East India Company and much of the shipping interest looked askance at measures to reduce the effectiveness of the Navigation Acts. Textile manufacturers, on the other hand, were anxious to increase still further the two-thirds share of Britain's export market they enjoyed in the 1820s (**4**, p. 394) and welcomed the new opportunities.

Most controversy attended protection for agriculture. The logic of the political economists' case pointed to a revision of the strongly protectionist Corn Law of 1815 (Chapter 4), yet the recent sharp fall in agricultural prices made it more difficult to follow a logical path. Wheat prices, which reached a post-war peak of 96*s* 11*d* (£4.84) a quarter in 1817, plummeted to 44*s* 7*d* (£2.23) by 1822. The talk was all of depression [**docs. 5 & 6**]. Huskisson, who as both an intellectual and an MP for the commercial constituency of Liverpool, never had rural backbenchers' confidence, talked of cheaper bread benefiting the 'labouring parts of the community' (**55**, p. 102). Sir John Sinclair spoke for the agricultural classes when he asserted that 'the cultivation of the soil . . . is the true basis of national prosperity' and that 'the interests of agriculture . . . ought never to be sacrificed for any considerations of distant commerce or of foreign policy' [**doc. 4**].

Despite strong pressure from agricultural associations and vigorous propaganda organised by the West Countryman George Webb Hall, the strength of the free-trade case within the parliamentary select committees was sufficient to negate calls for still higher protection. The 1815 Corn Law was mildly amended in 1822 to allow foreign corn into the country at graduated rates of duty when prices were between 70*s* (£3.50) and 85*s* (£4.25) and freely thereafter. It had no practical effect, however, since prices did not reach these levels while the law was in force.

A small circle of Liverpool's advisers, Huskisson, Canning, Peel and Robinson, all known to be sympathetic to the case for liberalisation, worked towards a more radical solution. The case for reform was strengthened when wheat prices rose sharply in 1826, following a poor harvest the previous year. The attractive political solution was a sliding scale of protective duties which would allow corn imports when domestic supplies were low and prices rising sharply, while keeping them out when the domestic harvest was adequate or better. Such a solution was less persuasive to the political economists. They argued that the absence of protection would stimulate rationalisation of agriculture and promote more market-conscious farming. Political considerations suggested caution and the revised Corn Bill on which Huskisson and Liverpool had been working was not carried until after not only the Prime Minister's death but that of his successor, Canning.

The 1828 Corn Law was passed by the Wellington government. It repealed the 1815 and 1822 statutes and substituted a sliding scale operating when the domestic price was between 60s (£3) and 72s (£3.60) a quarter. Corn could be imported freely when the price reached 73s (£3.65). Wellington, more sympathetic to the interests of backbench squires than Huskisson had been, increased the duty payable when the sliding scale operated above the rate proposed in earlier drafts on the Bill in 1826 and 1827.

Trade policy moved broadly, but cautiously, in more 'liberal' directions between 1819 and 1828. Though it is difficult to demonstrate cause and effect, most of these years were ones of prosperity. Tory-inclined journals, such as the *Annual Register*, were keen to link the improvement to the government's commercial initiatives [**doc. 7**]. The wisdom, liberality and moderation of government to which the *Register* referred, however, would have been challenged by a substantial proportion of the population. Moreover, tensions within the government ranks were very close to the surface in 1826–27. Among those tensions, as the years after 1827 would reveal, trade policy cut across social as well as political divisions. Despite its extraordinary intellectual dominance between 1820 and about 1860, free trade remained a deeply divisive issue.

11 Law, Police and Unions

English law in the early nineteenth century was ripe for reform.
The legal code, in theory extremely severe but in practice enforced
haphazardly if not chaotically, attracted increasingly stringent criticism. More than 200 offences carried the death penalty, though
this much-quoted statistic is misleading. The list of capital offences
contained many duplications; some identical crimes were
pronounced capital in statutes enacted at different times and
relating to different places. Capital punishment was rarely invoked
except for those crimes considered to be the most serious, but these
included both forgery and horse-stealing. Almost a third of all
executions in London and Middlesex in the early years of the nineteenth century were for forgery (**34**, p. 211). The severity of
punishments was almost certainly counter-productive. Juries were
frequently reluctant to convict even when the evidence was unas-
sailable. This was generally true of cases brought against food
rioters. Food rioting, common when wheat or bread prices rose
sharply, aimed at reducing prices to 'natural' or 'customary' levels
far below the temporary market price (**46**). Poaching, increasingly
an organised crime in the hands of local gangs, nevertheless
attracted community sympathy in times of distress or high prices,
since it ran foul of ferocious game laws. Convictions were less
numerous than the authorities liked.

The draconian punishments which rioters and poachers might
face emphasised the extent to which English law, made by property
owners, protected property first and foremost. This inherently
inequitable situation became positively dangerous when linked to
radical demands for political reform. The political thought of the
eighteenth-century Enlightenment stressed equality before the law
and, judged by this criterion, English law failed miserably. The
movement to reform the law and to improve conditions for convicts
gained influential support, not only from humanitarians like John
Howard or Whig intellectuals like Samuel Romilly and Sir James
Mackintosh, but also from those who argued more pragmatically
that a legal system which did not command popular consent could

not, for all its casual and arbitrary savagery, protect property effectively.

Sir Robert Peel was the ideal figure to carry through a programme of law reform in a Tory government. He was an exceptionally able and conscientious man whose talents were organisational and administrative rather than original and innovative. The English law required rationalisation and codification; some argued that it should be scrapped and totally remodelled. The radical plans of zealots like the great English philosopher Jeremy Bentham, who corresponded copiously with Peel in the late 1820s, would not have been acceptable to backbench MPs. Backbenchers sought a more efficient system, particularly since crime statistics showed an alarming rise after the end of the Napoleonic Wars. A parliamentary enquiry had unearthed the alarming fact that criminal commitments between 1809 and 1816 totalled 47,522 but had risen to 93,718 between 1818 and 1825, an increase of 97 per cent (**20**, p. 341). Criminologists and social historians tend to decry crime statistics, arguing that they are as likely to reflect fashions in prosecution or altered police attitudes as genuine changes in criminal behaviour. Whatever the truth of the matter, such statistics exerted a great visceral influence on contemporaries, as indeed they do to this day.

It is often noted that Peel's legal reforms were prompted by enquiries and reports made by the parliamentary committee of 1819 chaired by Mackintosh. It is less frequently observed that they took place during what contemporaries were convinced was a crime wave. Tory backbenchers and independent MPs hoped for more expeditious and effective justice to be meted out to wrongdoers. This impetus was probably at least as important a factor in the acceptability of Peel's work as was the influence of humanitarianism. For Peel himself, as the nature of his reforms demonstrates, neither factor weighed so much as did the desire to rationalise an outmoded and inefficient system.

The Gaols Act of 1823 had been clearly presaged by early initiatives and would not have been possible but for the tireless propaganda work of the Bedfordshire philanthropist landowner John Howard, who had seen the wretchedness of local prisons when acting as county sheriff and who had written his influential *The State of the Prisons in England and Wales* as early as 1777. The Gaols Act represented the first articulation of national policy on prisons. Each county and large town must now maintain from the rates a common gaol or house of correction. All such gaols were placed under a standard system of discipline with inspection by Justices of the Peace. The Act was extended in 1824 to include gaols in smaller towns. A system of classification of prisoners was also introduced (**20, 36**).

While disappointing some Whig and humanitarian reformers with his caution, Peel nevertheless saw five statutes through Parliament in 1823 which greatly reduced the number of offences carrying the death penalty. Larceny of property worth less than £2 was at last removed from the list of capital offences. These relaxations of the penal code were possibly partly because of thorough preparation within the Home Office. Peel relied much on the work of Henry Hobhouse, the diligent and experienced Under-Secretary he had inherited from Sidmouth. The political acceptability of this 'liberalisation', however, owed much to MPs' realisation that transportation was an ostensibly more humane but equally permanent way of ridding the state of its major transgressors. By the end of the 1820s, almost 5,000 convicts a year were being removed to the penal settlements in Australia. Almost a third of those convicted at assizes or quarter sessions, where the most serious cases were tried, were transported between 1810 and 1835 (**34**).

Peel even had some success in reforming the fiercely – some English critics said notoriously – independent Scottish legal system with a consolidating statute of 1825 which, among other things, clarified the rights of defendants. In 1825, also, the Jury Act rationalised more than eighty statutes, making the law on jury selection and responsibilities much clearer. He had only minor success in unblocking the encrusted and overloaded channels of the Court of Chancery. Here the caustic high-Tory Lord Chancellor, Eldon, who held the office with one brief break from 1801 to 1827, set a precedent for some of his successors in preferring longevity to activity.

In administrative terms, the most ambitious of Peel's legal reforms were the great consolidating statutes of 1826 and 1827. That of 1826 improved the administration of criminal justice while five statutes passed in 1827 rationalised ninety-two ramshackle, and in many instances unworkable, pieces of legislation into a credible code dealing with theft and injury to property, offences which accounted for about 85 per cent of all committals. While Home Secretary in Wellington's administration in 1830, he also passed a statute which reduced the number of cases in which forgery might be considered a capital offence.

In popular recollection, of course, Peel is the politician who introduced an effective police force. As so often, the truth is less dramatic and more subtle. The idea of a 'preventive police', whose functions would include not just catching offenders but deterring prospective criminals, had a long pedigree and as long a history of stern opposition. The parliamentary committee which Peel set up on becoming Home Secretary stated that 'It is difficult to reconcile an effective system of police with that perfect freedom of action and exemption from interference which are the great privileges and blessings of society in this country' (**6**, p. 287). This vigorous defence of traditional liberties was buttressed during the French Wars by news of the distasteful centralism which Napoleon was visiting on the French. The English country gentleman, more vocal in Parliament on such questions than on any others except the price of corn, had both a xenophobic and a pragmatic dislike of bureaucracy, 'codes' and controls.

Peel, who had helped to create a Police Preservation Force when Chief Secretary for Ireland, was better equipped than most politicians to see the advantages of professional policing but he did not envisage such forces outside London, whose population of 1.4 million in the 1820s was ten times as large as that of any other English city. Elsewhere until after the Municipal Corporations Act of 1835 the eighteenth-century system of local constables and watchmen survived. The onus of prosecution, if not necessarily arrest, was placed on the victim of a crime, not on the constable, so deterrence was very weak. London, however, had problems unique in scale if nothing else. They were highlighted by the rising crime figures. Only the historic City (with a mere 125,000 inhabitants) had a substantial force of watchmen and constables. Elsewhere in the capital, population had massively outstripped the means of policing. Some administrative adjustments had been made immediately after the end of the war and by 1818 the Home Office had direct control over the Bow Street police force. This, however, was not considered large enough to cope with major outbreaks of crime or disorder.

Peel expanded the Bow Street force in 1822 by appointing twenty-four uniformed officers (known as 'redbreasts' because of the colour of their tunics) to patrol central London by day. More extensive solutions were required. As in other areas, Peel advocated controversial changes obliquely by appointing Select Committees dominated by government supporters. An initiative at the end of 1826 was frustrated when Liverpool's government ended, but Peel took the issue up again on returning to the Home Office in February 1828.

The Committee's recommendation that a uniformed, professional preventive police be established in London was, of course, Peel's preferred solution and the Metropolitan Police Act of 1829 acted upon it. The Act created an entirely new organisation of five divisions under the control of two commissioners directly responsible to the Home Secretary. It was to be financed by a local rate. The police force of 3,000 recruited under this legislation was the first centralised force in the country. The City of London, which retained separate arrangements, was not included. In would be misleading to suggest that the Act produced overnight gains in policing efficiency or that the new constables were all models of incorruptible professionalism. Nevertheless, under the first commissioners, a retired army officer, Charles Rowan, and an Irish lawyer, Richard Mayne, impressive organisational progress was made in the 1830s. The administrative structure created in 1829 served as a model for the urban and rural police forces established between the mid-1830s and the late 1850s, and senior London officers became much in demand to run these provincial forces.

The legislation of 1824 and 1825 which repealed the Combination Acts and made trade unions legal did not result from massive protests by working people. Until the last quarter of the nineteenth century, unions were neither powerful nor specially important. Had they been so, it is doubtful whether Parliament would have consented to repeal. In fact, one argument used by Joseph Hume, the radical MP for Aberdeen, and Francis Place, an experienced London democrat from the 1790s who was also by the 1820s one of the capital's largest tailoring employers, was that only their continued illegality persuaded workmen to form unions.

Place rested his case not on labour solidarity but on orthodox political economy. J. R. McCulloch was one of many who argued that wages would find their natural level in a competitive market; they could not be raised above it by combinations of workers. Combinations might, however, fulfil the useful function of persuading reluctant employers to increase wages to the 'proper' market level (**44**, p. 285) and should anyway be permitted in a free society. *The Edinburgh Review* and *The Scotsman* lent support to the cause and the Combination Acts were repealed in a thin and apathetic House of Commons. The free traders in the Cabinet were generally persuaded, though repeal was a backbench not a government initiative. Huskisson supported it because 'the laws against combinations have tended to multiply combinations . . . they had generally aggravated the evil they were intended to remove' (**4**, p. 162).

The economic boom, however, proved Huskisson wrong. Unions of skilled workers sprang up in Lancashire, the north-east, the midlands and London as men attempted to capitalise on labour shortages. The hostile *Blackwood's Magazine* complained that these new unions (though, in reality, many were established Friendly Societies re-named unions) were 'filled with the worst spirit' and aimed 'to place the masters under the most grinding tyranny' (**44**, p. 286). Many did not survive the slump of late 1825 and 1826 but their activities sufficiently alarmed MPs to ensure the passage of an amending Act in 1825. Despite concern that the Combination Acts would be re-imposed, the new Act confirmed the legality of workmen's combinations 'solely for the purpose of consulting upon and determining the rate of wages or prices'. It did, however, spell out the illegality of any form of coercion or picketing. Prosecution under laws of conspiracy also remained a strong possibility (**42**).

The legislation of 1825, as later unionists were to discover, gave workmen little effective protection. Peel believed the amended law to be 'founded upon just principles' (**6**, p. 210). Workers should have the basic liberty to associate together. All of the stratagems which were likely to make unionism effective, however, were anathema. Significantly, Peel anticipated that the 1825 Act would put an end to 'the worst of the evils of combination' – by which he meant strikes and any form of disorderly behaviour. The repeal of the Combination Acts was more effective in satisfying the consciences of free-trade politicians with certain abstract notions of 'liberty' than it was in establishing trade unionism as a viable collective activity.

12   Foreign Policy under Canning

There used to be a fashion, which examiners happily followed, for contrasting the foreign policy of Castlereagh with that of his successor, George Canning. The fashion generally portrayed Castlereagh as the friend of established, autocratic regimes who, in pursuit of his anti-liberal objectives, involved Britain in close alliances with the crowned heads of Europe. Canning, though a staunch anti-reformer at home, was a supporter of liberal and national movements abroad who reverted to the normal peacetime tradition of keeping Europe, and its rival powers, at arm's length.

The fallibility of this view of Castlereagh was suggested in Chapter 7, and it will be argued here that the characterisation is of limited value even on the Canning side of the equation. Nevertheless, it is true that Castlereagh's 'Congress diplomacy' attracted widespread criticism not only in the radical press, which was to be expected, but also in the Cabinet, where none spoke more sharply than Canning whose aversion to Britain's participation in great-power meetings rested both on present needs and on Britain's historical avoidance of European entanglement [**doc. 10**].

Canning's reaction might be explained by envy of Castlereagh's success. Only a year apart in age, they had been personal rivals since the days of their political apprenticeships under the younger Pitt. Canning had made much the greater initial impact and had been Foreign Secretary in Portland's short-lived Tory administration as early as 1807 when he outranked Castlereagh. The two men had fought a famously-publicised duel in 1809 when Castlereagh accused Canning, not without justice, of trying to undermine his cabinet position as Secretary for War when the French War was going badly. It was beyond dispute that Liverpool's evident, and characteristic, preference as Prime Minister for Castlereagh's stolid dependability over Canning's mercurial and abrasive talents rankled with a man now forced to accept a less senior office than his rival.

However much politicians seek to deny it, opportunism and self-interest greatly influence their actions, and the real enemies of self-advancement are more often found within one's own party than in the ranks of the opposition. Canning's attacks on Castlereagh need to be seen in this context. Canning's much greater fluency as a parliamentary debater and his more assiduous concern about public opinion – he was perhaps the first major British politician to concern himself with cultivating a distinctive 'image' – emphasised the presentational contrasts between the two men. Beneath the presentation, however, the two men did genuinely differ over the likely benefits of Congress diplomacy. It is possible that the way events after 1820 seemed to vindicate Canning's view rather than Castlereagh's contributed to the latter's mental instability at the end of his life.

Britain was represented at the last authentic Congress, in Verona in the autumn of 1822, by the Duke of Wellington, the cabinet minister least in sympathy with Canning's approach to politics, though he recognised the necessity for his appointment as Foreign Secretary and did important work in persuading George IV not to block it. Wellington and Canning were in no serious disagreement about policy at Verona. Indeed, the guidelines drawn up by Castlereagh were adopted. Wellington helped to block Tsar Alexander's plans for combined allied intervention on behalf of the beleaguered Ferdinand VII of Spain and was also sufficiently wary of Russian intentions over the Greek rebellion (see Chapter 7) to draw closer to Metternich and the Austrians, thus confirming that the great-power accord of 1815–18 was obsolete. Canning after 1822 merely made manifest what was almost certainly clear to Castlereagh in 1821, that Britain must detach herself from general systems and seek alliances which best suited specific circumstances. 'Every nation for itself, and God for us all' is how Canning put it. Metternich personally detested Canning, calling him 'a world scourge' (**64**, p. 95), and he greatly exaggerated his 'liberality'. However, the two men acted harmoniously enough to ensure that the Greek rebellion was not exploited by the Russians to increase their influence in the Mediterranean.

The Congress System was finally killed at St Petersburg in 1825 when the Austrians and Russians failed to agree on a joint response to the Greek problem. Britain, which was not represented at St Petersburg, had recognised a Greek government in 1823, although Canning was more anxious to safeguard Britain's trading and strategic interests in the Mediterranean than he was to assert any nationalist priorities.

When the new Tsar, Nicholas I, showed a determination to

exploit Turkish weakness in Greece, Canning sought an agreement with the Russians, his primary objective being to avoid a Russo-Turkish war and consequent instability in the Mediterranean. Wellington was despatched to St Petersburg and a protocol between Britain and Russia was signed in 1826. This recognised an effectively independent Greece though under limited Turkish sovereignty. This was confirmed, with the addition of French signatures, as the Treaty of London in July 1827 (**4**, p. 414).

The treaty represented the peak of British influence over Greek independence. Less than a month after it was signed Canning died. The subsequent drift in foreign policy during the Goderich and Wellington administrations when the Earl of Dudley and the inexperienced Earl of Aberdeen were in charge allowed Russia to capitalise. An allied fleet under the command of Admiral Codrington soundly defeated the Turks at the Battle of Navarino in 1827, though the battle might well have been avoided with consequent advantage to European stability. The brief Russo-Turkish war which followed had more damaging consequences. It effectively destroyed the Anglo-Russian alliance and persuaded Wellington to believe that British interests lay rather in propping up the Turks. This policy was both unrealistic and unpopular at home. It implied a lessening commitment to the Greeks at a time when public sympathy for their cause was at its height. By the time the Greeks obtained complete independence in 1832, Russia had increased its influence in the Balkans, Britain's stock in the Mediterranean stood considerably lower than in the Canning era and her imperial and commercial interests in India and the Middle East were thereby threatened.

Important though the Greek issue was, Canning believed that the most decisive areas of British interest in the 1820s were the western Mediterranean and Latin America. Britain's relations with Spain and Portugal had strong strategic and commercial implications. Unhampered access to Mediterranean trade required stability on the Iberian peninsula, and Britain had traditionally strong links with Portugal. Spanish and Portuguese controls over the South American colonies they had ruled since the sixteenth century crumbled very rapidly early in the nineteenth. Canning made no secret of the fact that he intended to maximize the commercial opportunities thus presented.

Both Spain and Portugal were enfeebled countries in the 1820s. The Spanish constitution of 1812, never supported by King

Ferdinand, was overthrown with the aid of French troops in 1823, when Louis XVIII cited the agreements at the Congresses of Troppau and Laibach as warrant for intervention. Spain returned to absolutism. Canning, who was not in a strong position in Cabinet in his first couple of years as Liverpool's Foreign Secretary, allowed himself to be persuaded not to intervene since the Spaniards were divided and Britain's interests were not directly threatened.

Britain's involvement with Portugal was much greater. Indeed, British officers, under Viscount Beresford, had contained liberal forces in the country from 1816 to 1820 with the approval of King John VI who preferred to remain in the Portguese colony of Brazil. The liberals were successful in imposing a constitution on the King in the early 1820s although the country remained both economically weak and politically divided. After King John's death in 1826, the British sent 4,000 troops to Lisbon in support of a fleet of warships already in the Tagus. The purpose was to guarantee the stability of the existing government and to prevent Portugal from coming under domination by any other of the great powers. Canning wrote to the British ambassador in Lisbon that Britain had 'treaties of ancient obligation' which gave her 'a preponderance in the affairs of Portugal which . . . she has not the choice of abandoning' (**22**, pp. 412–3).

In reality, British intervention owed much more to concern with the balance of power than to any chivalrous considerations, and Canning was not slow to exploit a public opinion more liberal than the views of most of his cabinet colleagues. His speech of explanation to the Commons [**doc. 14**] was well received by the Whig opposition, while many Tories believed that Canning's real purpose was to weaken established authority and order.

Canning told Wellington soon after becoming Foreign Secretary that 'the American questions are out of all proportion more important to us than the European . . . if we do not seize and turn them to our advantage in time, we shall rue the loss of an opportunity never, never to be recovered' (**22**, p. 345). The opportunity referred to was primarily commercial. Buenos Aires, Colombia and Mexico, erstwhile Spanish possessions whose independence Britain recognised in 1824, and Brazil, recognised as independent from Portugal the following year, all became important in Britain's emerging 'informal empire'. Britain had no intention of annexing them as colonies but rapidly established herself as their leading supplier of manufactured goods. It was this commercial hegemony which Canning meant when, in welcoming the independence of the Latin American states, he declared that 'Spanish America is free; and if we do not mismanage our affairs sadly, she is English' (**63**, p. 169). Both the Manchester and the Birmingham Chambers of Commerce petitioned Parliament to recognise the independence of the Latin American states. It was a plea which Canning, who was for ten years an MP for Liverpool, Britain's largest commercial and industrial seat, was unlikely to ignore.

Canning's Latin American policy had strategic aspects also. In 1823, he extracted from the French ambassador, Prince Polignac, an agreement known as the Polignac Memorandum which pledged that France, now the dominant influence in Spain, retained no territorial ambitions in the New World. This chimed in neatly with the famous Declaration of the US President James Monroe in December 1823 that 'the American continents . . . are henceforth not to be considered as future subjects for colonization by any European power'. The Declaration offered no threat to Britain, whose future designs were commercial rather than colonial, and it unintentionally supported Canning's own strategy. In his own famous phrase [**doc. 14**], Canning 'called the New World into existence, to redress the balance of the old . . . if France had Spain, it should not be Spain "with the Indies"'.

The other strategic consideration has received less notice from European historians, but is probably the more important. Canning's Latin American policy was also designed to put a brake on US colonialism. Britain's commercial interests were supported by the British navy and this fact was probably sufficient to ensure that the United States confined its territorial claims to the north American continent. Canning laid great stress on the need to curb the 'ambition and ascendancy of the United States of America'. Two 'Great Powers' thus developed in the Americas. The USA was uneasily sandwiched between a British colonial presence in Canada and both a commercial and a colonial British influence in Latin America and the West Indies.

Canning took great pride in his Latin American policy, yet it is doubtful if it brought Britain quite the benefits he anticipated. It certainly did nothing to strengthen his own political position. Latin American nationalism was regarded as a strange, alien force by most of his cabinet colleagues. Wellington spluttered that Canning's policy had delivered the continent into the hands of 'revolutionary rascals and blackguards' (**28**, p. 46) and George IV's ancient prejudice against Canning was still further strengthened. Only in the last years of his reign did the King grudgingly respect Canning's vision.

Yet, visionary though his policy was, Canning grossly exaggerated the extent of immediate commercial benefit Britain would derive. Paradoxically, the great growth of Latin American trade was in the last decade *before* the spate of independence declarations, not in the first decade after. British exports to Latin America stood at £2.5 million in 1815 and £5.0 million in 1825. By 1835, they had hardly increased at all and had fallen back from 13 per cent of British exports to 11 per cent (**4**, p. 395). The new states were underpopulated and, until the advent of railways in the 1860s, had only rudimentary communication networks. They also developed their own basic domestic industries. The expectations of Birmingham and Manchester traders were frequently to be disappointed in Colombia, Mexico and Brazil.

Part Four: Stability Shattered 1827–32

13 The Break-up of the Tory Party, 1827–30

Although it is easy to discover portents in the preceding years (Chapter 9), the suddenness with which the Tory party fell apart after Liverpool's stroke in February 1827 amazed contemporaries. The society hostess Lady Cowper remarked in May that 'there is such confusion and splitting among families and parties that it is quite . . . a danger to talk politics at all, and yet it is impossible to talk of anything else' (**22**, p. 451). The protracted negotiations to form a new Cabinet involved disagreements within the Whig, as well as the Tory, party, though the Whigs survived them much better.

Some historians are reluctant to acknowledge parties as the central element in politics between 1815 and 1832 and they have cited the extraordinary confusion which followed Liverpool's resignation as evidence for their view (**5, 9, 79, 81**). The actors in the drama, however, invariably made party disunity its central focus, which they would hardly have done if politics had been conducted in 'non-party' forms while Liverpool was Prime Minister. It is surely better to see the period 1827–30 as one in which major shifts in existing party loyalties took place, rather than as an indicator of the looseness of party ties. Times of party fluidity are not uncommon in the longer run of British politics, as the years 1792–94, 1846–59, 1885–86, 1916–22 and, on the centre-left in our time, 1981–88, all demonstrate (**83**).

Such periods, of course, alter existing assumptions and perceptions. That discussed here brought radical parliamentary reform to the forefront of British politics in 1830 when five years earlier nothing would have seemed less likely. Nevertheless, the break-up of Liverpool's apparently unchallengeable anti-reformist Tory party had nothing to do with the franchise and much to do with those personal antagonisms and vanities which are so often the harbingers of political change. It had even more to do with religion. Students in a predominantly secular age are prone to overlook the raw, emotional power of religion as a political issue. Yet it was the Catholic question which had made Liverpool talk of resignation in 1826 and which precluded the formation of a stable Tory ministry after he had gone.

So dramatic are the changes which took place over the next five years that they have persuaded one historian that society and politics in England remained overwhelmingly Anglican, monarchical, authoritarian and deferential until 1828. Thereafter, hurricane-force winds, blowing unabated until 1832, destroyed the ancient edifice (**32**). Such an extreme view flies in the face of too much evidence, from the fact of the Industrial Revolution at one extreme to the contempt in which George IV was held at the other, to be persuasive as a whole. Yet it does indicate how much happened in this brief period.

George Canning had for some years been regarded by Liverpool as his natural successor, but Canning, though he had both experience and ability, lacked Liverpool's authority. He had two other disadvantages. His partisan nature and highly-developed talent for browbeating did not compel either respect or deference in colleagues of similar seniority. Wellington, in particular, loathed him. He was also the firmest supporter in Liverpool's Cabinet of Roman Catholic emancipation, a cause for which there was no marked public sympathy in Britain and much violent hostility within his own party. Although Canning had no intention of sponsoring an Emancipation Bill, he would not guarantee to oppose any such Bill if introduced by others. That degree of equivocation was enough to lose him the support of convinced Tory 'Protestants'.

Ironically, Canning's firmest supporter during the period of more than two months which it took to install him as Prime Minister was the King, once his most implacable enemy. George had grown closer to Canning, belatedly acknowledging that his Foreign Minister's policies were increasing national prestige. He saw no reason to depart from Liverpool's preference. Half of Liverpool's Cabinet, however, did. The 'Protestants', led by Wellington, Peel, Westmorland, Melville, Eldon and Bathurst, all refused to serve under Canning [**doc. 15**]. Wellington even quit as Commander-in-Chief. In all, about forty office holders resigned.

Canning did not have sufficient talent at his disposal among 'Catholic' Tories to fill the gaps, though he seized the opportunity to promote Viscount Palmerston, who had been Secretary of War since 1809, to his first cabinet post. Palmerston, the great survivor of nineteenth-century politics, would spend twenty-seven of the next thirty-eight years until his death in 1865 as a cabinet minister. Since the Tories who departed would not commit themselves to supporting a Canningite ministry, parliamentary arithmetic dictated an approach to the Whigs who, having been out of office since 1807, might have been expected to jump at any offer. In fact, there was much reluctance. Grey, whose personal hostility to Canning – at least as great as Wellington's – was mingled with snobbish disdain at a Prime Minister whose mother had been an actress, refused to have anything to do with an alliance and many Whigs took their lead from him.

Eventually, after hectoring from Brougham, who feared the return of a reactionary high-Tory ministry and whose principle, as he put it, was '*anything* to lock the door for ever on Eldon and Co' (**27**, p. 215), enough Whig support was pledged to allow Canning to anticipate Parliamentary majorities. Three Whigs, Lansdowne, Tierney and the Earl of Carlisle, joined the Cabinet. One discontented Whig asserted that Canning's elevation had 'dissected both Whigs and Tories' (**11**, p. 218). This was an exaggeration, but during the spring of 1827 political opinion had polarised on one large, and dangerous, issue – Catholic Emancipation – and on one controversial politician – Canning. Party labels became temporarily subordinate.

Canning, whose health had been poor for upwards of a year, declared himself 'quite knocked up' in July 1827 and died early the following month. Strain and the overwork involved in both heading an inexperienced government and acting as his own Chancellor of the Exchequer were contributory factors, though lung and liver inflammation was diagnosed. Given the difficulties which had attended the formation of Canning's government, George IV was reluctant to disturb its balance. He was also out of humour with the 'ultra' Tories whom he believed to have betrayed Canning. Thus, to preserve continuity, he turned to Frederick Robinson who had taken a peerage as Viscount Goderich after accepting Canning's offer to lead for the government in the House of Lords a few months earlier.

Goderich had extensive ministerial experience, having been in office continuously since 1809 (**24**). He had served Liverpool with quiet efficiency and had been fortunate to serve as Chancellor of the Exchequer during an economic boom (Chapter 10). What he had never shown, however, was leadership. His only virtue as Prime Minister in 1827 was that he permitted the delicate political balancing act which the Canning government represented to be maintained. He had the additional, but dubious, merit in George IV's eyes of allowing the King to exercise an influence over appointments which neither Liverpool nor, briefly, Canning had permitted.

The Goderich ministry was the last occasion in British history when the monarch ruled as well as reigned. His Prime Minister totally lacked conviction. He was unable to rally Whig support. The Whigs, for once rightly, feared royal influence and also believed, wrongly, that the return of Wellington as Commander-in-Chief indicated insidious high-Tory influence backstage. Goderich's ministry collapsed inwards in the autumn of 1827 when Huskisson, Lansdowne and Herries all attempted to resign. Goderich submitted a tearful resignation to the King early in January 1828, thus avoiding the embarrassment of having to defend his record before Parliament. He remains the only Prime Minister never to have faced a parliamentary session. The fact that his ministry lasted for almost five months indicates how brief parliamentary sessions usually were before the first Reform Act. Huskisson, Goderich's Colonial Secretary, believed that 'never, surely, was there a man at the head of affairs so weak, undecided, and utterly helpless' (**1**, p. 63).

Events in January 1828 left the King with no alternative but to turn back to the 'Protestant' Tories, and he could at least recognise the obvious. The day after Goderich's resignation, George invited Wellington to form a 'strong government' (**28**, p. 71) and Wellington, having a soldier's uncomplicated view about the evils which had beset the nation since Liverpool's resignation, had no qualms about accepting. The Whigs were not considered for office and Wellington's instinct was to dismiss the Canningite 'Catholics', led by Huskisson, along with them. Only Peel's insistence on strong debating talent in the Commons persuaded the new Prime Minister to keep them on.

The Tory ministry, therefore, initially looked similar to Liverpool's, but any expectation that it could establish an equivalent stability was rapidly disabused. The broader base lasted for only four months. From the beginning there was a lack of trust within the government. Wellington made no secret of the fact that he blamed Huskisson and the Canningites for contributing to the weakness of government in 1827 and, against Peel's advice, manoeuvred for an opportunity to get rid of them. He squabbled with them over levels of protection in the new Corn Bill (Chapter 10). They suspected him of trying to undo Canning's foreign policy

(Chapter 12), though Wellington had put one of their number, the Earl of Dudley, at the Foreign Office.

The eventual rift, in May 1828, occurred over a trivial disagreement about how to redistribute two parliamentary boroughs which had been disfranchised for corruption at the 1826 election. When his preference for giving the new seats to large boroughs rather than to the counties was over-ruled, Huskisson made what he believed to be a merely formal offer of resignation. He was surprised at the alacrity with which Wellington accepted it. Dudley, Grant, Lamb and Palmerston left with Huskisson and the resulting Tory ministry became unequivocally 'Protestant' in complexion.

This ministerial reshuffle had more profound consequences than either side could know. The Canningites rapidly made common cause with their recent Whig allies while Grey, who had stood aloof from Canning's entreaties in 1827, increasingly saw the value of a united opposition against what the Whigs believed to be an 'ultra' Tory government. Once the Canningites had accepted the necessity for Parliamentary reform, which in 1829 and 1830 they all did, the way was open for a permanent political realignment from which the Whigs derived great benefit. The Canningites would not take office in a Tory government again and the most durable of them, Palmerston, is almost invariably remembered as the greatest of the Whig Foreign Secretaries. His 'liberal Tory' origins are virtually forgotten.

In jumping from the Canningite frying pan, Wellington soon discovered that he had landed himself in that most intense of Tory fires – one stoked by religious bigotry. In a sense, his problem was that he was never the unbending 'Ultra' which the Whigs feared, and the real Tory 'Ultras' hoped, him to be. At the annual Tory Pitt dinner, Lord Eldon celebrated the departure of the Canningites as a victory for the Protestant Ascendancy. Wellington meanwhile tried to convince himself that 'this country was never governed in practice according to the extreme principles of any party whatever; much less according to extremes which other opposing parties attribute to its adversaries' (**28**, p. 80). The Ultras failed to heed the warning.

The reconstruction of Wellington's ministry itself led inexorably to a still more damaging Tory split. To replace Grant as President of the Board of Trade, Wellington chose an Irishman, Vesey Fitzgerald. According to the practice of the time, Fitzgerald had to resign his seat at County Clare and fight a by-election in his new guise as a Cabinet minister. Despite the fact that Fitzgerald was known to favour Catholic emancipation, Daniel O'Connell judged this to be an appropriate moment to bring his campaign to a climax. He stood against Fitzgerald in the County Clare by-election of July 1828 and won resoundingly. The victory brought the emancipation issue to crisis point, as O'Connell had planned. As a Catholic, he was debarred from taking his seat at Westminster, but he made it quite clear that the Protestant Ascendancy might expect violence if the law were not amended to enable him to represent his constituents.

Peel, who knew as much about Ireland as anyone in Wellington's Cabinet, counselled his chief that O'Connell could not be defied without risking civil war. Wellington had already raised the temperature there by dismissing the Chief Secretary for Ireland, the Marquis of Anglesey, for advising concessions. He now drew back from confrontation and prepared a Catholic Emancipation Bill (Chapter 14), although he had to risk dismissal by George IV in doing so.

Royal anger Wellington could discount. He knew that no remotely palatable alternative who could command parliamentary support was available. The Tory Ultras were another matter. Their fury was wondrous to behold. The Dowager Duchess of Richmond showed her contempt for Wellington's 'ratting' on his Protestant commitments by festooning her drawing room with stuffed rats labelled with the names of ministers (**74**, p. 54). Sir Robert Peel resigned his seat at Oxford University and was defeated by Tory 'Protestants' when he recontested it. He had to take a pocket borough to remain in Parliament. The Marquis of Winchilsea charged Wellington in *The Standard* newspaper with hatching a cynical plan for the infringement of Englishmen's liberties and 'the introduction of Popery in every department of the State' (**20**, p. 581). Winchilsea and Wellington fought a duel over the accusation at Battersea Fields in March 1829.

Canningite and Whig votes meant that Wellington was in no danger of parliamentary defeat over Catholic emancipation, but the 173 Tory backbenchers in the Commons and the 109 peers who voted against him in the Lords in March 1829 placed a time bomb under the ministry. The Ultras would not be mollified; some were even converted to parliamentary reform in the misguided belief that only the government's rotten boroughs had thwarted popular anti-Catholic sentiment (Chapter 16). Between the spring of 1829 and the autumn of 1830 Wellington's government was on long notice of ejection. The Tory party was shattered into three feuding groups. The Canningites by mid-1830 were all but committed to the Whigs. Wellington and Peel were finding out how long the centre could hold. The Ultras fumed, fulminated and plotted against leaders by whom they felt betrayed. The cause of parliamentary reform was greatly advanced by these decisive splits in Liverpool's anti-reform party, but it was religion rather than wider representation which had brought them about.

Economic discontent added to the government's difficulties from late 1829 onwards. Rejuvenated and more broadly-based extra-parliamentary pressure for reform surfaced (Chapter 15). The death of George IV in June 1830 necessitated a general election. Wellington hoped to use it, in the time-honoured way, to strengthen his position in Parliament by use of government patronage (**77**). His electoral fire was directed at Canningite MPs, whom he believed to be vulnerable. He was mistaken. The Canningite Charles Grant defeated a government challenger at Inverness. The Home Secretary's brother, Jonathan Peel, was beaten in the large and relatively democratic borough of Norwich [**docs. 26–28**] and Wellington also lost one of the government's more eloquent journalistic supporters, John Wilson Croker. The election did not produce overwhelming anti-government majorities; as usual before 1832 few seats were actually contested. The consensus was that the government made only a small net loss but its psychological effect was substantial.

The election, and the European revolutions which also took place in 1830 in France, Belgium and Poland, convinced more wavering MPs of the need for concessions on parliamentary reform. The Whigs were encouraged to raise the issue again. Wellington's own conviction remained anti-reformist but, after Catholic emancipation, Ultra backing was uncertain. His famous speech in early November [**doc. 29**], asserting that the existing franchise and distribution of seats had the entire confidence of the country, was, therefore, foolhardy, even considered within a Westminster perspective. In the country as a whole, the judgement was ludicrous. Wellington's error – he plaintively enquired of the Earl of Aberdeen on sitting down, 'I have not said too much, have I?' – was seized on by Whigs and Canningites. With Ultra support, they engineered a government defeat on a minor issue but one which Wellington had intimated he would consider one of confidence in his government. His resignation followed immediately. A Whig government took its place, pledged to parliamentary reform. The Whig backbencher, Sir Robert Heron, summed up the rapidity with which events had changed: 'Two years ago, I thought Reform of Parliament almost hopeless. I now believe it to be certain and approaching' (**74**, p. 100).

14 The Religious Question, 1828–29

The bare facts about the two major religious reforms of the period are simple. In February 1828, after concerted action by leading nonconformists and some younger members of the Whig party, Lord John Russell sponsored a motion in the House of Commons calling on MPs to consider the validity of existing legislation which barred Protestant dissenters from holding any office in local or central government. The Test and Corporation Acts had been passed in 1673 and 1661 respectively when an ostentatiously dominant Church of England was regarded as an essential bastion of strength for the restored monarchy of Charles II after the dark days of Cromwell and the English republic. Many republicans had been inflexible and dogmatic dissenters, as much opposed to bishops as to kings.

Nonconformists had always been permitted to sit in Parliament though not to hold office. Since the Hanoverian succession, the practical disabilities imposed by the Test and Corporation Acts had gradually diminished; many blind eyes had been turned and many indemnities issued by the authorities. Yet the Acts remained, symbolic of second-class citizenship. Many eighteenth-century attempts at repeal had failed before the French Revolution postponed all libertarian reforms. Now Russell's motion was passed by a clear majority in the Commons and, when it reached the Lords, the bishops were not disposed to block it. Robert Peel had done some careful lobbying, securing the support of the two archbishops and four leading bishops (**32**). Bishop Lloyd of Oxford asserted that the laws encouraged mere pretence of Anglicanism by influential citizens; their repeal would encourage honesty and true religion. A hasty amendment by the Bishop of Llandaff kept public office closed to Jews, atheists and agnostics but, otherwise, anti-dissenting Ultra Tories received no encouragement from the episcopal bench, where they might most have expected to find it (**6**). The Acts were repealed by a Protestant Tory government under Wellington with very little parliamentary opposition.

As has been seen (Chapter 13), the passage of Roman Catholic

Emancipation was much more contentious and produced great bitterness within the Tory party. Nevertheless, a Tory government in February 1829 sponsored a Bill to repeal all penal laws against any of His Majesty's Catholic subjects in Great Britain or Ireland [**doc. 25**] Like the Test and Corporation Acts, most of the relevant anti-Catholic legislation had been passed towards the end of the seventeenth century, in 1678 during the 'Popish Plot' and in 1689 when Protestant ascendancy was institutionalised by statute in the 'Glorious Revolution'. Most of the 'persecuting' legislation against Catholics in England had been repealed in 1791, though they were still debarred from holding public office and also from voting and sitting in Parliament. Catholics had been permitted to vote for members of the Irish Parliament in 1793, seven years before the Act of Union, and these voting rights were transferred to the United Kingdom Parliament, along with Ireland's one hundred MPs, in 1801.

Roman Catholic emancipation was hedged by two qualifications. The arrival of Catholic MPs was accompanied by a sharp increase in the county voting qualification in Ireland from 40*s* (£2) to £10, thus removing the anyway remote possibility of a mass peasant vote in that country. O'Connell's Catholic Association was also formally suppressed in order to appease those who thought his organisation an affront to law and order. This was mostly window-dressing, however, since the Association had been established primarily to secure that which its Tory opponents now conceded. Given the virulence of anti-Catholicism in England, the two-to-one vote by the Lords in favour of emancipation in April 1829 was surprising. It shocked the King who believed himself 'deserted by an aristocracy which had supported his father' (**32**, p. 398). That the King's trenchant and well-publicised opposition could so easily be overborne was a clear indication that the power of the monarchy had evaporated. Protestant Ultras, equally aghast at what they saw as a fundamental act of betrayal and a supine con-cession to the forces of 'revolution', were left to plot their revenge against Wellington and Peel (Chapter 13).

It is tempting to see both pieces of reformist legislation in 'Whig-gish' terms. Those historians who see the unfolding of the past in broadly progressive terms have no difficulty in explaining these important concessions as part of a gradual awakening to liberal toleration which was the hallmark of a mature and successful people. Since religious bigotry, in their eyes, was essentially benighted, so the changes of 1828 and 1829 symbolised progress.

Historians working in the 1970s and 1980s have seen sufficient examples in their own time of religious zealotry and bigotry alive and well and living almost all over the globe to be sceptical of what might be called the 'progressivist' model of religious change. Accordingly, they have been critical of two assumptions about the religious legislation of 1828–29 (**31, 32, 59, 87, 90, 91**). The first is that these Acts are best seen as a tasty *hors d'oeuvre* to the more significant 'achievement' of parliamentary reform in 1832. The second is that the Ultras were ignorant, bigoted and purely reactionary folk with no coherent philosophy, only a set of unpleasant 'gut assumptions' which were, quite rightly, challenged and defeated.

Contemporaries who opposed the religious reforms of 1828–29 regarded them as a 'treason' greater than that which took place in 1832. Only in the context of later political reforms which culminated in a full, democratic franchise can the importance of 1832 be properly gauged. Such a perspective was not available to the Marquis of Winchilsea, Lord Eldon or any of the Tory Ultras who felt so keenly betrayed by Wellington and Peel. Their historical perspective, naturally, derived from the seventeenth and eighteenth centuries when religion was the most important determinant of political attitudes. It was to remain so for most of the nineteenth century. While the changes of 1828 and 1829 weakened the case against political reform, therefore, this was less immediately important for defenders of the Anglican establishment (which, before 1832, meant defenders of the existing political as well as religious settlement) than the unwise concessions which the state was making on religion. As John Cannon has written, 'One of the most essential features of the old constitution was the identification of Church and State, dovetailed together under aristocratic supervision' (**31**, p. 102).

Thus for conservatives on the religious question, concessions weakened not only church but state [**doc. 24**]. Eldon considered repeal of the Test and Corporation Acts 'a manoeuvre in favour of Popery, carried on under cover of liberality to the Dissenters'. When the Catholic Bill was considered the following year, he appeared in the unlikely guise of tribune of the people, playing expertly on the populist anti-Catholicism which made emancipation, even in England, a much livelier issue than repeal of the Test and Corporation Acts:

'The people were justly attached to the constitution of 1688 [the

Glorious Revolution which installed Protestant William III in place of Catholic James II]; they looked to it as the foundation and bulwark of their freedom. If a part were changed, there might be a change in the whole; and that change they dreaded' (**32**, p. 398).

In the context of the early nineteenth century, it is easy to demonstrate that the Ultras did indeed have a coherent position. It will not do to dismiss them as faintly absurd backwoodsmen who vainly strove to hold back the inexorably reformist tide of history. Yet this is what has frequently been done. When society was urbanising rapidly (Chapter 2) and the centre of economic gravity was shifting from south to north, they represented rural England in general and the arable south and east in particular. When both dissent and Catholicism were making impressive strides (see below) in the urban north, they defended the supremacy of Anglicanism from communities in which the Church of England remained both overwhelmingly dominant and well-served by its clergymen. When political economists preached free trade and the supreme social and economic arbitration of the market place, the Ultras defended protection for land as the pre-eminent form of property. They also asserted the organic unity of a society founded on an established hierarchy which recognised paternalist values.

It is not necessary to agree with the Ultras in order to understand their philosophy. To deny its structural coherence is to accept that history is indeed the propaganda of the victors. In one sense, the alleged Tory 'backwoodsmen' of aristocratic England are in as much need of rescue from 'the enormous condescension of posterity' as were England's lower orders before Edward Thompson both rehabilitated and romanticised them (**48**). A critical reading of the Tory house journals *The Quarterly Review* and *Blackwood's Edinburgh Magazine* does not show either to be the intellectual inferior of the Whig *Edinburgh Review* or the radical-Benthamite *Westminster Review*. Their real crime was to have lost the argument to superior economic forces in a rapidly industrialising society. History forgives such 'crimes' less readily than it should.

The preceding paragraphs are not an apologia for the Ultras, merely a plea for disinterested appraisal of their position. It is not necessary to resort to economic determinism to discover why, on the religious issue, they lost so decisively. Wellington and Peel were fearful that refusal to grant emancipation would lead to civil war in Ireland (Chapter 13). Even in England, however, Catholicism was gaining strength. From a small base among the gentry of the north-west since the late sixteenth century, Roman Catholicism doubled in strength between 1800 and 1830. Almost half the Catholic community, furthermore, was located in the thriving Lancashire commercial and industrial towns of Liverpool, Manchester, Preston and Wigan (**4, 31, 57**). Catholicism was a much more important force in English society than it had been since the Reformation.

Dissent, too, after many years in the doldrums in the first half of the eighteenth century, was picking up. The 'old dissent', represented by Presbyterianism, Congregationalists and Baptists, increased its combined membership by about 77 per cent to 743,000 between 1800 and 1830. The Methodists, more recently established, increased their membership by more than three times to about 300,000 in the same period, though divided into warring sects after John Wesley's death. Methodists, it is interesting to note, were much more anti-Catholic than most nonconformist sects in this period and did not campaign actively, as did the older dissenting groups, for repeal of the Test and Corporation Acts (**4, 58, 91**).

Overall, it was difficult for Peel and Wellington to deny first, that dissenters offered no evident threat to public order in Britain; second, that they were growing substantially in numbers; third, that their contribution to trade, commerce and industry was disproportionately strong; and fourth, that existing legislation was the more anomalous when religious plurality was an established fact in England, Scotland and Wales. Continued Anglican hegemony required more special pleading than either thought it prudent to attempt. Only in the hectic years between 1829 and 1832 did the force of the anti-reforming case become more apparent. Looked at through Tory eyes, it seemed that the government was not making judicious concessions over marginal issues: it was destroying the ideological basis of the old order. The changes of 1828 and 1829 should be considered as an integral part of the history of reform, not as a prelude to it.

15 Economic Distress and Political Organisation, 1829–30

Events in Parliament between 1827 and 1830 seriously weakened the anti-reformers, but the background to parliamentary reform cannot be understood only from Westminster. Politicians during the reform crisis of 1830–32 constantly referred to public opinion and to the extent of disaffection 'out of doors'. Radical pressure for reform intensified at the end of the 1820s. Its revival owed something to the higher food prices which resulted from deficient harvests in 1829 and 1830 and something to trade depressions. Cobbett's dictum that only people with empty stomachs were receptive to radical political argument, though an obvious exaggeration, had basic validity. Reform flourished against a background of hardship. Nevertheless, it should be remembered that the economic crisis of 1826, though shorter, was sharper and was not accompanied by any significant radical revival.

Two other factors, however, were at work. Pressure on behalf of working people became both more extensive and more confident in these years as the lessons of past failures were assimilated. Also, middle-class activity reached new levels of intensity, partly for intellectual and partly for economic reasons. The writings of Jeremy Bentham and the Utilitarians had drawn pointed attention to the irrationality of a political system which offered no uniform voting franchise, and which gave underpopulated and economically stagnant Cornwall forty-four seats in the House of Commons while buoyant Lancashire had only fourteen (**74, 76, 77**).

Some middle-class opinion, also, was dissatisfied that economic growth was so frequently punctuated by periods of sharp recession, accompanied not only by unemployment but also by widespread bankruptcies. The textbook accounts of these years, which now stress a growing 'working-class consciousness', usually fail to notice the extreme volatility of middle-class entrepreneurship. Only the largest and most fortunate employers survived periods of recession. A glance at trade directories of midland and northern towns over ten-year periods shows how fast was the turnover both of factory owners and master manufacturers. Never was business such a hazardous activity as in the first half of the nineteenth century.

It is frequently observed that the reform crisis saw a conjunction of middle- and working-class pressure against the aristocracy. This observation is over-simple in itself, since it assumes that a coherent middle class and a coherent working class existed in 1830–32. Neither did. It also fails adequately to explain the reasons for middle-class dissatisfaction with the existing political structure. The obvious inequalities pointed out by Benthamites and by artisan radicals only take us so far. Birmingham and Manchester businessmen had long voted in the country constituencies of Warwickshire and Lancashire, and had exerted considerable influence in the selection of county members there (**15, 32**). They were not, therefore, 'unrepresented' in the old system. What needs much greater emphasis is the *economic* incentive for political change. Business, though potentially extremely profitable, was highly uncertain and an important section of the middle-class came to believe that the level of risk had much to do with government policy.

Fierce debate, which divided middle-class opinion, raged about the reasons for the apparent inefficiency of the economy. The classical political economists (Chapter 10) looked no further than existing restraints on freedom of trade and commerce. When these were removed, unfettered economic growth was confidently expected. Others, of whom the Birmingham banker Thomas Attwood was the leading exponent, emphasised 'underconsumption'. This theory held that full employment and maximum productivity could be guaranteed only when the amount of currency in circulation matched the productive capacity of the economy. Since orthodox economic policy now dictated balanced budgets, currency restrictions and free trade, it challenged this theory at almost every point.

It was but a short step for Attwood's followers to agree with the artisan radicals (Chapter 4) that high taxes set by a landowners' Parliament were used to support the government's army of place-holders and 'stockjobbers'. Indirect taxation on basic necessities like foodstuffs reduced the potential for domestic consumption. People were paying so much in indirect taxation that they had insufficient surplus to buy manufactured goods in the quantities needed to sustain the livelihoods of businessmen and labourers alike.

Thus was forged a potent alliance between one section of the middle class and much the most articulate and literate section of working people – the artisans – to secure a political remedy for economic grievances. The common target was 'Old Corruption' and the struggle was characterised as one between the 'productive' and the 'unproductive' classes of society. Such a characterisation was a travesty of the truth, but the point about political slogans is not whether they are true (which is rarely the case) but whether they are believed (which they frequently are). True or not, the alliance alarmed parliamentary opinion as it had not been alarmed since a French invasion seemed imminent in 1797. Unlike 1797, or even 1819, however, far fewer MPs now believed that the appropriate response should be further repression.

Unease about the continued viability of the political system was increased by the 'Swing Riots', which broke out in the late summer of 1830 and continued until the autumn of 1831. These disturbances (named after the mythical Captain Swing whose name appeared at the bottom of threatening letters, and who was supposed to be the movement's leader) took place in the rural south and east of England where, despite previous disorders in 1816 and 1822, levels of popular political consciousness were far less high than in London or the industrial towns. 'Swing' was a movement of labourers and rural craftsmen brought to the edge of despair by recent price rises in a society afflicted by structural under-employment and a consequential downward pressure on wages.

More than 'hunger politics' was involved, however. Labourers were selective in their targets. Threshing machines, which threatened one of the few sources of winter work, were destroyed; the hay ricks of farmers who paid wages below the local odds were set aflame. Among the 1,400 or so reported 'Swing' incidents were many examples of community activity against local leaders accused of failing to discharge traditional obligations (**37**). Clergymen who, in their dual capacity as Justices of the Peace, fined or imprisoned local poachers, and Poor Law overseers who adopted harsh or inquisitorial methods, were likely to receive threatening letters or to be burned in effigy (**4, 88**). The Swing Riots were a violent assertion that paternalism, which many MPs saw as the foundation of a social and political order dependent on hierarchy and reciprocal obligations, had broken down. Thus was a political message conveyed in sub-political ways.

In the towns, more structured collective activity was taking place in the late 1820s, especially among the skilled workers. John

Doherty used the greater scope provided by the repeal of the Combination Acts (Chapter 11) to organise the cotton spinners of Lancashire and Cheshire in an effective union before the combined effects of trade depression and concerted employer opposition caused its collapse in the autumn of 1829. Doherty responded with a 'Grand General Union of Operative Cotton Spinners', active in 1829 and 1830, and then with his real objective, a workers' union across the trades. The 'National Association for the Protection of Labour' was founded in September 1829. Though it recruited overwhelmingly from the textile trades, it claimed about 70,000 members at its peak in 1830. Doherty used the potential of general unionism to advocate political reform in his trades journal *Voice of the People* in 1830 and 1831 (**44**).

Co-operation also grew very rapidly between 1825 and 1830, partly as an alternative strategy when strikes collapsed. By 1830, about 300 co-operative trading associations were in existence with about 20,000 members (**7, 38**). Robert Owen, who returned to Britain in 1829 after the failure of his co-operative community of New Harmony in Indiana, encouraged co-operators, especially in their growing links with trade unions. By 1832, a Union Exchange Society had been established for workers to swap the products of their labour without resort to an entrepreneur, and the National Equitable Labour Exchange had been established in London where the trading currency was the 'labour-value note' rather than orthodox currency.

Implicitly or explicitly, co-operation involved educating working people to the potential of collective action, and the opportunity was not lost by the co-operative journals. The leading theorist of co-operation in these years was Dr William King, who had been a Fellow of Peterhouse College in Cambridge before moving to Brighton, where he helped to establish a Mechanics' Institution. Between 1828 and 1830 he edited *The Co-operator*, which attacked the wastefulness of capitalist competition. The first edition asserted: 'At present we work one against another – when one of us gets work, another loses it'. The lesson was clear: 'Let us therefore begin to work for OURSELVES ... Every member of the Society will work, there will be no idlers. All the property will be common property'.

Co-operation, not surprisingly, had the greatest attraction for those in permanent work. It thrived for a few years among the London artisans. William Lovett and James Watson, both of whom later helped to draft the Democratic People's Charter, founded the

Co-operative Magazine and helped to establish the British Association for promoting Co-Operative Knowledge in 1829. *The Weekly Free Press*, edited by William Carpenter and John Cleave, also advocated co-operation. By mid-1830, more than forty co-operative societies were known to exist in the capital and about 500 throughout the country were known to the association early in 1831 (**70**).

The resurgence of political radicalism in London was threatened by routine squabbles among its leaders. The Radical Reform Association, founded by Hunt and Cobbett, was riven with disagreement. Hunt favoured a direct attack on the old political system; Cobbett preferred currency reform and went off to tour the country in support both of his favoured solution and a seat for himself in Parliament. Richard Carlile had become even more strident in his hatred of priests and in his advocacy of self-improvement through education and discipline. He attacked the new Association's lack of intellectual rigour. He harangued his hearers in his journal *Lion*: 'You cannot be free, you can find no reform, until you begin it yourselves . . . abstain from gin and the gin-shop, from ale and the ale-house, from gospel and the gospel-shop, from sin and silly salvation' (**65**, p. 198). The lectures given by Carlile and his more scurrilous and less scrupulous colleague Richard Taylor at the Rotunda in Blackfriars Road in the summer of 1830 attracted large crowds. They raised the political temperature during a year of distress in the capital (**70**).

By the autumn of 1830, London was also reacting to a new French Revolution in Paris, which put the revival of 'liberty politics' into a European context for the first time since the French wars. Since March it had also had a Metropolitan Political Union, formed by Hunt with support from Daniel O'Connell, which called for 'a real Radical Reform'. This organisation was a response to the establishment two months earlier of the Birmingham Political Union. The success of the Birmingham organisation emphasised, as had much extra-parliamentary pressure since 1815, the growing importance of the urban provincial centres in national political life (**43**).

The political unions are often held to have generated and sustained, by an insistent petitioning campaign in 1830 and 1831, that critical extra-parliamentary pressure without which no Reform Act would have been passed. Thomas Attwood, the founder of the Birmingham Political Union, claimed in January 1831 that his organisation had 'condensed the moral power of this great population, and gathered it ... into an electric mass, which was powerful to every good purpose'.

The motivations of the Whigs in passing reform are considered below (Chapter 16) but it is important to stress here the diverse nature of the political unions. The Birmingham Political Union – 'a general political union between the Lower and the Middle Classes of the People' formed to achieve 'an effectual Reform in the Commons House of Parliament' (**74**, p. 60) – was hardly the model for a national agitation. It was established only when a petition for currency reform (Attwood's hobby horse) was denied, and its radical critics insisted that Attwood remained more interested in currency than in democracy.

Though he claimed much for its later influence, Attwood had no initial intention of using the BPU as a model for other political unions. Its middle-class leaders, in fact, were representatives of a local Tory group who opposed 'Whig' political economy. The early activities of the Union were publicised only in the Tory-controlled *Birmingham Journal*. The Metropolitan Political Union, drawing on a deep vein of artisan awareness, had a more democratic programme. Concerted pressure encompassing skilled workers, manufacturers and commercial figures was much easier to sustain in towns like Birmingham, which retained small workshops, an apprenticeship system and personal relations between masters and men, than in factory towns. Thus, while Sheffield developed a union of similar social structure to Birmingham's, the Manchester Union, organised by Archibald Prentice, the radical editor of the *Manchester Times*, drew support mostly from the intellectual middle-classes and from skilled workers rather than from cotton manufacturers or labourers. In Leeds, three separate unions emerged with little in common.

The cumulative effect of these various activities, warring and contradictory though many of them were, outweighed their many shortcomings. By the time that Grey took office the overwhelming feeling 'out of doors' was that the old political system neither could nor should be sustained. More alarming to MPs at Westminster was the range of interests apparently reaching similar conclusions. A landowners' Parliament could not risk flouting middle-class opinion. The belief that continued resistance to reform would provoke violence and the forcible imposition of a democratic political structure persuaded many MPs to support parliamentary reform, though more out of fear than conviction.

16 The Return of the Whigs and the Reform Crisis, 1830–32

The government formed by the second Earl Grey in November 1830 was from the first agreed that a measure of parliamentary reform was essential. This conclusion did not fulfil some manifest historical destiny; it was a reaction to short-term political developments. The combination of growing extra-parliamentary pressure (Chapter 15) and the instant focussing of opinion on the issue as a result of Wellington's anti-reform pronouncement [**doc. 29**] made it inconceivable that it could take any other course.

The government was not uniformly enthusiastic either about the immediate prospect for reform or the longer term consequences if a Reform Bill negotiated the parliamentary minefield without being blown up. Grey's reputation is that of a long-term reformer, but he had hardly been staunch in the cause. More important, many senior Whig ministers, notably the Home Secretary, Viscount Melbourne, and the Lord President, the Marquis of Lansdowne, were paternalist landowners who saw reform, at best, as a necessary nuisance. The prospect of increasing the political influence of the midland and northern towns they regarded with Olympian distaste. They silently shared the prejudices of the Tory backbencher Horace Twiss who in 1831 lamented the prospect of calling in 'shopkeepers and attorneys, persons of narrow minds and bigotted views . . . to counsel the nation' (**76**, p. 215).

Furthermore, the government was described as 'Whig' only for convenience. It was in reality a coalition between the old Whig landed connection and the Liberal Tories who had left Wellington and Peel in 1827 and 1828 (Chapter 13). Their leader after the death of Canning was William Huskisson, who had never been on close terms with the Whigs. During the last, tottering, months of Wellington's administration, Grey and Lansdowne believed that Huskisson would prefer to refashion a broader Tory governing group rather than unite with the Whigs. In any event, Huskisson's tragic death in September 1830, the first casualty of a steam train accident, eased negotiations between the Liberal Tories and the Whig grandees. In November 1830, therefore, Palmerston happily accepted the Foreign Office and Grant the Control Board. These Huskissonites could see the need for some constitutional changes. Palmerston, in particular, had been influenced by the recent revolution in France (**96**). By no stretch of the imagination, however, could the Whigs' coalition partners be called fervent reformers. They had been followers of Canning who, whatever his other liberal predilections, had never been a parliamentary reformer.

A further complication presented itself in the self-regarding and irascible shape of Henry Brougham. Brougham had won a well-publicised victory in the country constituency of Yorkshire at the General Election of 1830, advancing what he called 'the great cause of parliamentary reform' (**27**). Brougham had long been the leading Whig spokesman on legal and humanitarian reforms. Adding the franchise question to his bulging quiver of 'issues' seemed like a hostile pre-emptive strike to colleagues already resentful of his ambition and suspicious of his motives. In 1830, he told Grey, he had a Reform Bill all ready to present to Parliament.

Grey could not keep his disliked colleague away from the Lord Chancellorship in his new administration, but he was determined not to be bounced into a parliamentary reform of Brougham's devising. The delicate task of formulating the Bill for presentation to Parliament in the spring of 1831 was given to a small committee of four from which Brougham was deliberately excluded. Its chairman was Lord Durham, Grey's brother-in-law. Lord John Russell, third son of the Duke of Bedford, earned his inclusion because of his experience with the Bill to disfranchise small boroughs which he had launched in 1822. Lord Duncannon was another prominent member of a landed Whig family who would inherit substantial estates as the Earl of Bessborough in 1844. Sir James Graham, less well-heeled but already marked out as a sound young man with important connections to the Huskissonite camp, was the fourth member (**74, 76, 96**).

This blue-blooded committee was selected in part, no doubt, to convince country gentlemen that the Whigs could be trusted to remember where the solid propertied interests of Britain lay. In the event, it was the commoner Graham who wanted fewest changes in representation. Initial worries were also allayed by Grey's emphasis on continuity in the exercise of power and on property as the necessary basis for the exercise of political influence. He wanted 'a greater influence to be yielded to the middle classes who have made wonderful advances both in property and intelligence, and this influence may be beneficially exerted upon the Government' (**96**, p. 64).

The nuts and bolts of the first Reform Bill were discussed in great secrecy, first within the committee and then by the Cabinet. The committee had favoured the introduction of a secret ballot and also the reduction in the maximum time between general elections from seven years to five. Grey squashed both proposals. The secret ballot was dismissed as 'unmanly' and 'unEnglish'. Nevertheless, the boldness of the Bill presented to Parliament in March 1831 shocked MPs [**doc. 34**]. It proposed the partial or total disfranchisement of 107 boroughs and the redistribution of 163 seats to the main urban centres of population and to the most densely populated counties. A uniform franchise was proposed for the boroughs, which would give the vote to householders occupying property valued for rental purposes at £10 a year or more. Some extensions to the county vote were also proposed, though the 40-shilling land freehold remained the basic franchise.

No one knew by how much this would increase the electorate, but any measure which proposed to remove the parliamentary constituencies of a quarter of existing MPs was bound to be highly controversial. Althorp said that he saw Peel turn 'black in the face' as he listened to Russell's speech in defence of the reform proposals. Even moderate reformers were taken aback: 'They were like men taking breath immediately after an explosion', Brougham's secretary Denis Le Marchant reported (**74**, p. 163). The debates on the first Bill saw opponents defend the historical integrity and efficiency of the existing composition of the House of Commons, while reformers urged the importance of a wider franchise to gain the confidence of increasingly important sections of public opinion. In these debates, the Whig backbencher and historian Thomas Babington Macaulay made his reputation as a great orator [**docs. 32, 33 and 35**]. The Commons had never seen such a large division as on 22 March 1831, when the Bill's second reading was passed by a single vote, 302 to 301.

This vote precipitated the next, and constitutional, phase of the reform crisis. Such an equal division of opinion in the Commons guaranteed defeat for the government when the detailed proposals were considered in committee. This duly occurred at the end of April, once the opposition forces had had time to re-group. Grey could either persevere with a diluted Bill or request the King to dissolve Parliament and call a general election. William IV had supported the Whigs to this point, but he required persuasion verging on coercion to agree to a dissolution of a Parliament still less than one year old. The forthcoming election, moreover, could be nothing less than a plebiscite on a particular issue. The political nation would be asked simply to declare for or against reform. The King knew that general elections on one 'issue' were exceedingly rare and of doubtful propriety, especially when Parliament had more than six years to run. He was persuaded by Durham to dissolve for fear of widespread public disorder if he resisted, but he extracted a pledge from ministers that, if they won, no more radical clauses would be inserted in the Bill.

The 1831 election produced the anticipated massive pro-reform majority. In almost all constituencies where voting was open enough to test propertied public opinion, reformers swept the board. Only the counties of Shropshire and Buckinghamshire returned two anti-reforming Tories. More than a third of the eighty-two English county members had declared against reform in the debates of March and April 1831. Only six re-appeared after the election (**74**). The Duke of Devonshire's agent wrote to the Duke that, even in the Ashbourne and Wirksworth districts of Derbyshire, traditionally considered one of the most conservative parts of the county, 'nine-tenths of the freeholders have declar'd for reform' (**82**, p. 425). The Tories had held about sixty seats in the larger, 'open' boroughs in the 1830 election; two-thirds of them were lost in 1831. The government's majority stood at between 130 and 140, guaranteeing a smooth passage for the Reform Bill in the Lower House.

The Upper House was a different matter. Here the hereditary peers, not needing to concern themselves with the tiresome and demeaning chore of elections, could exercise their opinions free of constraint, or so most of them thought in the autumn of 1831. A new Bill, similar to its predecessor in all essentials save one, passed the Commons in September 1831, piloted skilfully, as in March, by Althorp and Russell. The exception was the addition to the franchise of £50 tenants-at-will. This was at the instigation of two anti-reformers, the Marquis of Chandos and Colonel Charles Sibthorp, who saw in the enfranchisements of substantial tenants a means whereby 'legitimate' landed influence could be preserved in county seats. It was widely assumed (though subsequent research has not necessarily confirmed the impression) that tenants would support their landlord's candidate for fear of eviction. The 'Chandos Amendment' was significant. It increased the county electorate by about 30 per cent more than the Whigs had originally intended.

On 8 October, the Lords threw out the amended Bill by a comfortable majority of forty-one and precipitated the second stage of the constitutional crisis. Public opinion was already heavily committed to reform, although the more perceptive working-class leaders already realised how little ordinary folk might expect from it (**48, 70, 74**). The effects of economic depression and higher food prices (Chapter 15) had already provoked some disturbances. In June a full-scale riot (its historian calls it an 'armed insurrection') broke out in the South Wales iron town of Merthyr Tydfil. For several days the town was held against the troops by reformers; more than twenty people were killed in the conflict (**50**). It was a bloodier and more serious affair than Peterloo and deserves wider notice than it has received.

The authorities might, therefore, have anticipated popular reaction to the Lords' rejection of the Bill. Their anxieties were fully justified. The Duke of Newcastle's castle at Nottingham was burned during a riot in the city. Derby endured rioting crowds. Bristol was held against the authorities for three days at the end of October; the Bishop's palace and several gaols were sacked before order was restored. In many places, anti-clericalism was apparent, twenty-one of the twenty-six bishops having been decisive in securing a majority against reform in the Lords [**docs. 36 and 37**]. Perhaps more significant than the disturbances, which excessive quantities of drink exaggerated in their later stages, was the enormous growth of support for the political unions (Chapter 15) and the discovery of plans, which alarmed men like Attwood as much as they did Melbourne, for the collection of arms and for drilling. In London, Francis Place acted as midwife for a new National Political Union while the National Union of the Working Classes, also based in London, petitioned the Lords to grant universal manhood suffrage and annually-elected parliaments.

As the temperature rose, established and 'respectable' political unions in some towns became less confident of their ability to control pro-reform forces. *The Times* asserted that the troops were not sufficient to deal with 'occasions of sudden and very general emergency. We say then to our fellow subjects – organise and arm' (**74**, p. 253). By November 1831, the prospect of a total breakdown of public order appeared real. Cabinet disagreements surfaced and

Grey contemplated resignation in order to let Wellington try to persuade the recalcitrant Lords to pass reform when the Whigs had failed.

Sterner counsels prevailed and a fresh Reform Bill was presented by Russell in mid-December. It differed little from its predecessors, except that horse-trading provided some reprieves for small boroughs and a second seat was given to a few of the new boroughs to counterbalance the anticipated growth of landowner influence via the Chandos Amendment. In its final version, the Reform Bill deprived fifty-six English boroughs of representation; thirty more lost one of their two members. Seventy-seven new borough seats were created, sixty-three in England, eight in Scotland, four in Ireland and two in Wales. County seats in England and Wales were increased from 92 to 159 (**4**, p. 379, **77**, pp. 44–48).

The prospect of re-fighting a battle so recently lost disheartened the Cabinet in the early months of 1832. Grey had great difficulty in preventing wholesale resignations. Success in the Lords was far from assured, and some feared that the recent disturbances had stiffened the resolve of the diehard opponents of reform rather than the reverse. Durham was the first to support the creation of sufficient Whig peers to carry the measure. This third deviation from the unwritten constitutional code, following the premature dissolution of Parliament and a 'one-issue' election, was too much for William IV. When the Whigs were defeated on an amendment in the Lords early in May, Grey, having been refused fifty new Whig peers, resigned. The Tories under Wellington were charged by the King with the responsibility of trying to form an administration which would carry some sort of reform. Grey confided to a friend: 'Never was a captive more desirous of escaping from prison than I am from my present situation' (**76**, p. 234).

Wellington's attempt lasted less than a fortnight. It foundered largely on Peel's refusal to join a government which would have to pass reform. Peel, knowing what damage had been done to his career in 1829 (Chapter 14), feared that association with parliamentary reform in 1832 would kill it. Of more moment, however, was the enormous extra-parliamentary outcry that the prospective return of Wellington caused. Hostile petitions flooded into Westminster. The political unions organised massive demonstrations and threatened civil disobedience. Place devised a scheme for reformers to withdraw deposits from the banks simultaneously: 'To stop the Duke, go for Gold'. Protest marches from the northern and midland towns to London were organised [**doc. 39**]. It is unlikely that these 'Days of May' altered the course of events but they confirmed the tenacity of extra-parliamentary agitation during the reform crisis.

After Wellington's admission that he could not form a government, resistance to reform crumbled. The King was forced to promise new peers as a condition of Grey's return, but they were not needed. Most of the Tories absented themselves from further debates in the Lords and the Bill was quickly carried. The King made a final, impotent, gesture on 7 June 1832 by refusing to attend the House of Lords to give the royal assent in person. It did not matter. The most dangerous political crisis of modern times was peacefully resolved.

The consequences of the Great Reform Act lie outside the scope of this book and have been considered elsewhere (**4, 77**). Some debate has taken place, however, about the true intentions of the Whigs in passing the Reform Act. Early twentieth-century students of the Act concluded that the Whigs had made judicious concessions to popular pressure (**29, 75**). Karl Marx, curiously, saw the Act not as a concession to pressure but as a party political stratagem intended to increase Whig patronage at the expense of the Tories (**95**). The most celebrated attempt to modify the traditional picture has come from D. C. Moore who saw the Act not as a concession to pressure, but as a 'cure' which, by clever manipulation of electoral boundaries, was intended to solve problems of conflicting influence. Those without property remained excluded from political influence, but the distinctions between county and borough seats were intended to prevent 'seepage' of middle-class commercial influence into the county seats. The increase of county representation was a means of retaining landed influence after 1832 (**13, 94**).

The Moore thesis is ingenious but it is too calculating by half. The Whigs, as we have seen, were anything but united. They did not have the statistical or psephological evidence to make fine calculations about relative middle-class or landed influence in the different types of constituency. Undoubtedly, they wished to dismantle the unstable, but potentially disastrous, alliance between middle and working classes. They were entirely opposed to democracy and firm in their determination that property and not numbers should retain decisive political influence (**5, 77, 96**). Beyond that, there was no consensus. Lacking a master plan, the Whigs had little alternative but to react to popular pressure. In the crisis of 1831–32 the passage of *some* reform bill was more important than arcane juggling over what, and who, was to be included and excluded. The Great Reform Act was an imperatively necessary concession to pressure which otherwise threatened to destroy not only a political system but an entire culture. Its intentions were conservative. It was left to Grey's successors to ponder at leisure how successful his concessions had been.

Part Five: Conclusion and Assessment

The main title of this book, *Britain before the Reform Act*, should not be taken to suggest that the years 1815–32 be read as some kind of extended prelude to the major change in the franchise enacted in 1832. The Great Reform Act was, of course, a watershed. In the short-term crisis that preceded it, Britain came closer to revolution (at a time, be it remembered, of European revolutions) than at any time in the eighteenth, nineteenth or twentieth centuries (**4, 77**). Parliamentary reform must, therefore, bulk large in any study of this period. It was, however, part of a much wider change which can only be appreciated by looking in some detail at the whole of the period 1815–32.

Britain's ability to effect a massive political and social transition in the first half of the nineteenth century without revolution had important implications for its development in the next century and a half. Some critics argue that Britain actually *needed* a revolution to pull it out of an attitude towards ancient institutions and traditions at once self-satisfied, sentimental and superior. What might be termed a culture of complacency grew up which deprived the country of a crucial cutting edge in world competition. Thus it is not self-evidently true that Britain's avoidance of political revolution in the early industrial period was, to use Sellar and Yeatman's magically simple phrase in *1066 and All That*, 'a good thing'. With that debate we are not concerned, though students should know that it exists.

The preceding pages have tried to demonstrate that political reform was by no means the only issue on the agenda between 1815 and 1832. To those contemporaries who opposed radical change, it took second place to religion as the issue on which the ending of the old world of deference and authority turned. Liverpool and his ministers gave close attention to questions of taxation, government debt, overseas trade and commercial policy. These issues much more directly affected the lives of most contemporaries than did debates about rotten boroughs and the political status of Manchester or Birmingham. Debates in Parliament concentrated on these questions and on foreign policy rather than on parliamentary reform, at least until 1831.

Past events and controversies need to be seen, as far as possible, from the perspective and understanding of those who lived through them. History is not, or should not be, the story of progress from a lesser to a greater state which can be plotted almost as a line moving steadily upward on a graph. The cruder varieties of such writing have been termed 'Whig history'. The phrase is intended to be dismissive. In fact it traduces a generation of meticulous and imaginative scholars from the late nineteenth century whose work is no longer much read (hence the crude facility with which it can be misleadingly parodied), but who laid secure foundations for the emergence of history as a scholarly profession in the twentieth century.

The phrase 'Whig history', though misused, should properly warn against concentration on issues only in the context of their significance for later generations. Thus 1832 should not be studied as one of a progression of dates which, with 1867, 1872, 1884, 1885, 1918 and 1928 charts the emergence of a democratic franchise. In its time, the first Reform Act is best characterised as a consciously anti-democratic measure. One of its main purposes was to frustrate the plans of working-class radical leaders for an assault on the citadels of privilege from which would emerge a democratic franchise and government by what they termed 'the productive classes'.

Contemporaries – a few atypical individuals like Major John Cartwright, Henry Hunt, and T. J. Wooler apart – were not obsessed with parliamentary reform between 1815 and 1832. Earl Grey, whose government eventually passed the measure, and who had introduced earlier reform motions in 1793 and 1797, thought reform a confounded nuisance from the end of the French Wars until about 1829. He believed that it had split the Whig party and, on more than one occasion, prevented its return to office. Even William Cobbett, the best-remembered radical writer of the age and a staunch proponent of parliamentary reform, offered his readers other targets than the restricted franchise. He lambasted the government for the savage and inhumane consequences of a currency policy which harmed the employment prospects and lowered the wage levels of working people. His famous attacks on the 'bloated' Church of England and his defence of the rural poor were not invariably linked to his case for democracy.

Ordinary folk, it is safe to assume (then as now), were much more concerned with material matters like the size and purchasing power of family incomes and the prospects for employment, than they were with the heady rhetoric of representation served up by Orator Hunt. The obstacles in the way of political literacy were substantial. The poorer areas of early industrial cities, where lived the great majority of urban citizens, were citadels of squalor, festering and pustulant affronts to a civilised nation. Mere survival was an achievement. It was an achievement, moreover, denied to about a quarter of the children born in British cities in the 1820s. Naturally, in such an environment, 'hunger politics' had an immediate appeal. The sustaining of any kind of deeper political consciousness required discipline, dedication, self-education, and self-denial of an order which compels admiration irrespective of one's political views.

In addition to issuing warnings against the fallacies of Whig history, historians have of late placed less stress on 'important dates'. This development has generally been welcomed by students since it places a lower premium on the memory training necessary to recall them, and a good thing too! Dates can always be looked up; however, a developed sense of chronology – a very different matter from 'learning dates' – is both a higher-grade skill and intrinsically more important than knowing that the Battle of Waterloo was fought in 1815 rather than 1814. This book, it will be recalled, began by urging that the importance of 1815 be not exaggerated. It ends with a plea to understand 1832 in its contemporary context. It is perhaps proper to add a codicil to rectify the revisionist balance somewhat.

Historians study the process of change over time. Even in such a short period as 1815 to 1832 changes took place of critical importance in understanding the transition from what might be termed the 'old' world of hereditary privilege, localism, paternalism and protection to a 'new' order encompassing representation of interests, liberalisation, free trade and an increasing role for central government. The new order stressed economic growth as essential to feed and find employment for a population which was growing much more rapidly in the first thirty years of the nineteenth century than ever before. It believed trade liberalisation to be the only way to secure growth. Industrialisation provided a greater diversity of wealth, not only in urban but also in rural society. A balance needed to be achieved between interests which would otherwise conflict. A more complex society eventually required both more government and greater direction from the centre.

The new order responded to the quickening pace of life. It is of more than symbolic importance that this period witnessed the opening of the world's first passenger railway. Those who opposed the Reform Act did so only in part because they disliked its specific terms; they had a deeper reason for opposition. The old political system, they believed, had grown both mystically and organically. It had been fought for in the seventeenth century, had achieved stability in the eighteenth and should not be tampered with on the coarse warrant of calculations about Birmingham's population or the number of MPs whose constituencies were in Cornwall. To amend was to destroy.

In one sense, the 'die-hards' were right. Though it was necessary to assert that the Reform Bill was 'the final solution of a great constitutional question' in order to persuade parliamentary doubters to support the measure, neither Russell nor Grey believed their own rhetoric. It was ludicrous to suppose that Manchester should return two Members of Parliament, but not three or four, until the last syllable of recorded time, or that the social composition of that collective representational artefact, the ten-pound householder, would remain unimpeachably respectable as election succeeded election and the value of money fell. As the Bill's opponents well knew, what had once been amended could be changed again as circumstances, or pressure, dictated. On this line of argument, and despite all the assurances of the Bill's supporters, 1832 was indeed the thin end of the democratic wedge.

A similar train of thought had guided opposition to the religious concessions of 1828–29. To grant political equality to dissenters or the vote to Catholics was to imply that the state church was, at best, first among equals. These reforms, opponents argued, removed protection for the Church of England, and Ultra-Tories had a strong aversion to free trade in faith on both historical and practical grounds. The primacy of a distinctively Anglican church had been a sure stronghold against Catholic insurgents and foreign invaders since the reign of Elizabeth I. Not only had it earned the continuing protection of the state; Ultras believed in the mystical bond between church and state. Their cosmos was sustained by dual, and equally weighted, pillars. Pull down one, and the edifice collapsed.

It is possible even here to find some justification for Ultra fears. Toleration for Dissenters and Catholics was further extended when the ancient universities were opened to them in the 1870s. By the end of the nineteenth century, toleration, if scarcely yet respectability, had been extended to atheists and agnostics. Though the conclusion is open to the charge of Whiggish determinism, that secularisation which is characteristic of the modern British political and social order might be traced back to crucial decisions about the nature of the relationship between church and state made by Wellington and Peel in 1828–29.

Political decisions on both Catholic Emancipation and political reform were strongly influenced by extra-parliamentary pressures. This is perhaps the most significant indicator of the transition from the old political world to the new. If Parliament was seen to bow to pressure 'out of doors', then the doctrine of 'virtual representations', by which the old world set such store, was fatally undermined. This doctrine held that all interests were 'virtually' represented in a legislature which put the wider national interest before selfish or class-based considerations. All that was needed to agitate the pure, if narrow, stream of political accountability was a steady flow of parliamentary petitions which brought local grievances to public notice for appropriate action and redress.

This doctrine reeked of preciousness and it had been mercilessly exposed in lampoons and satires from the middle of the eighteenth century onwards. Radicals believed that it had been killed by the self-interest of landowners when they introduced a fiercely protective Corn Law in 1815 which artificially inflated prices to consumers while helping to preserve aristocratic rent-rolls. Nevertheless, virtual representation retained vitality in Tory circles until the disasters of 1828–32. To concede to threats was fatal to the old concept of representation and also a sign of weak government. In Ultra eyes, the government acted under duress both in 1829 and 1832 and thus legitimated forms of unrepresentative extra-parliamentary action. Modern political structures recognise extra-parliamentary pressure groups and, though the Anti-Corn Law League of the late 1830s and early 1840s offers the best-developed example, earlier precedents can be found in the work of O'Connell's Catholic Association in the 1820s and in the provincial political unions of 1829–32.

It would be foolish to assert that what has been termed 'the new order in politics and society' emerged fully-developed and triumphant between 1815 and 1832. The old political world proved remarkably tenacious for at least another half-century after 1832, most notably in the continued power exercised by the landed classes and in the measure of 'influence' which landowners enjoyed at parliamentary elections (**4, 20, 40, 77**). We are, after all, discussing peaceful transition not violent change. Apocalyptic Tory visions – 'The reform bill is a stepping stone in England to a republic' (J. W. Croker); 'We shall be destroyed one after the other . . . by due course of law' (Wellington) – seem on the face of it only to confirm the follies of those who dared to obstruct the march of progress.

Facile jibes, however, are out of place. Grey and Russell, even more obviously than Croker and Wellington, were representatives of a long-established but introverted social and political world based on great wealth (mostly landed), family connection, deference and clientage. Over the course of a half-century or so, that world was slowly strangled. The life was choked out of it by the pressures of modernity. These were the social consequences of revolutionary industrial change; part and parcel of this was an increasingly sophisticated extra-parliamentary political consciousness. The student looking for the origins of the new order must look, not just to the reform crisis but to the teeming and turbulent years after 1815. The years covered by this book witness the birth of a new age.

Part Six: Documents

document 1
Lord Liverpool defends the Corn Law

*The imposition of a strongly protective tariff in 1815 was the subject of much criticism. It is generally depicted as class legislation enacted by a landowners' Parliament. Liverpool here argues that protection is in the interests of consumers as much as producers. Compare this defence of protection with the Liverpool government's moves towards freer trade in other areas [**doc. 8**]*

Lord Liverpool ... now came to the principle of the Bill, with respect to the policy of rendering ourselves as independent as possible of foreign supply ... It was not a question in this case as to the interests of the English landlord or the Irish landlord .... The great object was the interest of the Consumer; and this, he contended, would be effectually promoted by the present measure, the effect of which would be to render grain cheaper instead of dearer. The important point to attain was a steady and moderate price ... where the supply was fluctuating, a year of extraordinary cheapness of grain must necessarily be followed by one of dearness, unless measures were adopted to insure a regular domestic supply, and by this means a uniform steady and moderate price.

Hansard, 1st series, vol. xxx, col. 181, 15 March 1815

document 2
A Petition against the Income Tax, 1816

The government sustained an embarrassing defeat over its attempt to keep income tax in peacetime. Lord Althorp, Whig MP for the county of Northamptonshire from 1806 to 1832, here presents a petition drawn up not by him but by his constituents.

Lord Althorp, on presenting the petition from the borough of

Wellingborough, in Northamptonshire, against the property tax ... said, he was particularly instructed to support that part of the petition which referred to the pledges of economy given in the Speech from the throne at the opening of the session. He therefore invited the House to the most strict and rigid system of economy, as the only means of saving the country. He was aware that it might not be possible to satisfy the wishes of the people, groaning beneath their burthens, by any practicable reduction that was consistent with the honour and safety of the nation; but he was convinced, at the same time, that great savings might be made, and that it was the duty of the House to carry them immediately into execution.

Hansard, 1st series, vol. xxxiii, col. 123, 11 March 1816

document 3
George IV considers dismissing Lord Liverpool

This letter was never sent. It must be read in the context of the developing crisis over the Queen Caroline divorce case and it indicates, beneath a veneer of civility, how disenchanted the King had become with his ministers for, as he considered it, failing him on a vital matter. It is a draft reply to what, in normal circumstances, would have been a purely formal request from Prime Minister to monarch to prorogue Parliament for the Christmas period.

16 November 1820

THE KING will no longer delay acquainting Lord L. with the result of the deep and anxious consideration he has given to the measure of prorogation so strongly pressed upon the King by Lord L. The King acquiesces in this measure ... But it would not be at the same time consistent with that honor and fairness, with which the King has always acted towards his confidential servants, if the King were not to declare to Lord L. that, however painful it may be to the King's feelings, he considers himself under the necessity of taking measures for the formation of a new Administration.

A. Aspinall (ed.), *The Letters of George IV*, 3 vols, Cambridge, 1938, vol. 2, p. 380

document 4
Sir John Sinclair defends the agricultural interest

This is an extract from an address delivered by the President of the Board of Agriculture to the landlords and farmers of Great Britain. Its immediate context is the depression of arable prices. Notice the extravagance of Sinclair's language and his plea to the government to consider land as a special form of property.

The crisis has at last arrived; and the question now at issue, is, whether the agricultural interests, forming, with those of the various classes dependent on British agriculture, by far the most important part of the community . . . are to be sacrificed, to gratify the wild speculations of dealers in foreign corn . . . or the mercantile and manufacturing enterprises of foreign traders . . . . It is not to be doubted, that commercial and manufacturing industry, when resting on, and combined with, agricultural prosperity, cannot be too much promoted; and this union of the three branches [land being the third] has been the means of elevating Great Britain to such a height of power as has rarely been equalled. But, on the other hand, those endless, and often ruinous speculations in manufactures and foreign commerce, which cannot be successfully carried on *without the depression of British agriculture*, ought not to meet with the slightest legislative encouragement . . . . to render this country permanently independent of foreign supplies, the means of promoting the extension and improvement of agriculture shall be considered the *most important department of government*.

Farmers' Magazine, vol. xxiii, 1822, pp. 22–3, 46–7

document 5
A regional statement on the agricultural depression

This is an extract from the quarterly report on the state of agriculture county by county published in the Farmers' Magazine. *Compare its message and its tone with those of Sir John Sinclair* [**doc. 4**] *and the Earl of Thanet* [**doc. 6**]. *This article was written for publication in a magazine read overwhelmingly by landowners and the larger farmers.*

Our Corn markets have been, and still are, ruinously low; and, without any prospect of a considerable advance; many have been obliged to thrash out, and turn their corns into money at any price they would bring. Stock of every kind being proportionably low in price, has brought the farmer low in circumstances; and many respectable agriculturalists, who were lately considered as opulent, are now selling off to prevent utter ruin, or are sold up by their landlords under a distress of rent. So many and frequent are the instances of such distress, that it has become a common topic of conversation – 'Who will fall next?'

Quarterly Report for Buckinghamshire, *Farmers' Magazine*, vol. xxxiii, February 1822, p. 121

document 6
An unsympathetic view of the agricultural depression

The Earl of Thanet was a prominent Whig landowner. Here he writes in a sardonic tone to Thomas Creevey, the diarist and MP for Appleby, which constituency he represented on Thanet's patronage.

I am just returned from Kent, more disgusted than usual at the language and temper of those I saw, which I take for a sample of the rest; everybody complaining, without an idea that they could do anything towards attaining relief. Landlords and farmers seem to have no other occupation than comparing their respective distresses. They ask what is to happen. I answer – you will be ruined, and they stare like stuck pigs. I could not hear of one Tory gentleman who had changed. One booby says it is the Poor Rate – another the Tithe – another high rents – all omit the real cause, taxation, the mother of all evil.

Earl of Thanet to Thomas Creevey, September 1822, H. Maxwell, (ed.) *The Creevey Papers*, 2 vols, John Murray, 1904, vol. 2, p. 51

document 7
The Annual Register celebrates British commercial advance

The Annual Register, *as its name implies, provided a yearly review of major events together with a critical commentary.*

Fifty years ago, an economist, who should have ventured to predict the present developement [*sic*] of English commerce, capital, revenue, or debt, would have been laughed at as the most frantic of a visionary tribe; and it is by no means impossible that the next half century may work perhaps even a greater change than that which the preceeding one has witnessed. A whole hemisphere of the globe has, within the last ten years, been in a manner opened to our industry – an event of magnificent promise, and which may ultimately change the aspect of the civilized world. All the relics of the commercial code, constructed with such perverse ingenuity by our barbarous ancestors – for such, in these matters, may we consider the statesmen of the eighteenth century – are fast being demolished under the new enlightened policy of their present successors; and we cannot but be assured, that the wisdom of this change of system will yearly make itself more sensibly felt in the progressive expanding developement of the unrestricted energies of our trade.

Annual Register, vol. lxvi, 1824, p. 5

document 8
William Huskisson explains the value of tariff reductions

This document is taken from a speech delivered by Huskisson in the House of Commons when he was President of the Board of Trade and thus responsible for the formulation of commercial policy. Notice how Huskisson tries to disarm possible criticism of his trade liberalisation policy.

We furnish, in a proportion far exceeding the supply from any other country, the general markets of the world, with all the leading articles of manufacture, upon which I have now proposed greatly to lower the duties. I own that I am not afraid of this country being overwhelmed with foreign goods. Some, I know, will come in ... but they will not interfere with those articles of more wide and universal consumption, which our own manufacturers supply cheaper and better; whilst they will excite the ingenuity of our artists and workmen to attempt improvements, which may enable them to enter the lists with the foreigner in those very articles in which he has now an acknowledged superiority.

Speeches of William Huskisson, 3 vols, London, 1831, vol. ii, pp. 344–6, 25 March 1825

document 9

An attack on free trade

It is easy to lose sight of the fact that the economic philosophy of laissez-faire, though it became dominant in the 1820s and 1830s, attracted many critics. Such critics are not to be dismissed as cranks or reactionaries merely because their views did not win. The document comes from a much longer discussion of the impact of free trade on the labouring classes. It was written, not by a radical politician urging parliamentary reform, but by a Tory defender of protection and paternalism. Read it in conjunction with document 8.

There is indeed nothing in the conduct of the advocates of Free Trade so deserving of reprehension, as the hypocritical pretences with which they attempt to disguise or conceal the real object of their measures. If we credit their professions, this amiable and enlightened tribe of philosophers has nothing in view but the common good, and the improvement of the condition of the industrious classes. There is, however, room to think, that they overestimate the ignorance and blindness of the community in supposing that the mass of our population can be much longer hoodwinked by this flimsy pretence . . . Recent and dear bought experience has taught the working classes, that the free competition of foreign labour *must* diminish the compensation which they can expect to receive for their toil. The artisans and mechanics of this country have probably by this time become pretty well convinced, that the importation and consumption of the produce of foreign labour has no tendency to ameliorate their condition and that they at least form no portion of that public whom the Free Trade system is said to benefit.

Blackwood's Edinburgh Magazine, vol. xxvii, 1830, p. 561

document 10
Canning's reservations about the Congress System

This letter was written to Castlereagh – in Aix-la-Chapelle for the Congress of 1818 – by Lord Bathurst, Liverpool's Secretary for War and a close associate of Wellington. It reveals Canning's disquiet over Congress diplomacy and, as so often with Canning, it reflected a wider public unease.

Downing Street, 20 October 1818

The objections which Canning feels on this subject are not confined to the inexpediency of announcing a decision of meeting at fixed periods, but to the system itself . . . He thinks that system of periodical meetings of the four great Powers, with a view to the general concerns of Europe, new, and of very questionable policy; that it will necessarily involve us deeply in all the politics of the Continent, whereas our true policy has always been not to interfere except in great emergencies, and then with a commanding force. He thinks that all other States must protest against such an attempt to place them under subjection; that the meetings may become a scene of cabal and intrigue; and that the people of this country may be taught to look with great jealousy for their liberties, if our Court is engaged in meetings with great despotic monarchs,- deliberating upon what degree of revolutionary spirit may endanger the public security, and therefore require the interference of the Alliance.

Marquis of Londonderry (ed.), *Correspondence, Letters and Despatches of Lord Castlereagh*, 12 vols, London, 1853, vol. xii, pp. 56–7

document 11

The Castlereagh State Paper of May 1820

This much-quoted document marks Castlereagh's official recognition that Congress diplomacy was not working as he had intended. He had had a very different 'System' in mind from that envisaged by Tsar Alexander I and this Paper reasserts the need for pragmatic responses. It can also be read as a response to Canning's reservations, expressed in 1818 [**doc. 10**].

The principle of one State interfering by force in the internal affairs of another, in order to enforce obedience to the governing authority, is always a question of the greatest possible moral as well as political delicacy, and it is not meant here to examine it. It is only important on the present occasion to observe that to generalize such a principle and to think of reducing it to a System, or to impose it as an obligation, is a Scheme utterly impracticable and objectionable. There is not only the physical impossibility of giving execution to such a System, but there is the moral impracticability arising from the inaptitude of particular States to recognize, or to act upon it.

H. Temperley and L. M. Penson (eds), *Foundations of British Foreign Policy, 1792–1902*, Cambridge, 1938, p. 61

document 12
The benefits of close relations with South America

Prefaces to the Annual Register *in the early nineteenth century highlighted what the editor considered to be the most important political themes for a given year. His selection of South American diplomacy for 1825, therefore, needs to be read as a commentary on the importance of Canning's policies in the area.*

While the greater part of the Continent exhibits an aspect little cheering to the friends of the human race, consolation may be found in contemplating the state of England and the course of events beyond the Atlantic. Throughout the South American continent, not only has the cause of independence been victorious in the field, but some progress has been made in the establishment of regular government, and in laying the foundations of those institutions upon which well-ordered systems of freedom may be erected hereafter. Relations, too, of amity and commerce, with every likelihood of permanence, have sprung up between the new states and the parent and guardian of freedom in the old world, which must exercise a most beneficial influence both on their moral and on their political destiny.

Annual Register, vol. lxvii, 1825, p. v

document 13
Canning briefs the Consul-General of Buenos Aires

This document is dated 10 October 1823. It neatly encapsulates the main points of Canning's South American policy. Note Canning's anxiety that Britain's representative in this newly independent state should stress his country's commercial, as opposed to imperial, concerns. Note also the implication in the final sentence that Britain could be a guarantor of Spanish American liberties.

It may be unnecessary to state to you, but it is very material, that it should be understood by the persons with whom you communicate in Buenos Aires; that so far is Great Britain from looking to any more intimate connection with any of the late Spanish Provinces, than that of friendly and commercial Intercourse, that His Majesty could not be induced by any consideration to enter into any engagement which might be considered as bringing them under His Dominion. Neither, on the other hand, would His Majesty consent to see them (in the event of their final separation from Spain) brought under the Dominion of any other Power.

Public Record Office, F.O./6/1, Letter of Instruction, quoted in H. R. Ferns, *Britain and Argentina in the Nineteenth Century*, Arno Press, New York, 1977, p. 111

document 14
Canning's reasons for intervention in Portugal

This document should be read alongside documents 10 and 11, where the role of Britain in Europe is also debated. Canning saw British intervention in Portugal as necessary not only to bolster the government of a long-term ally but also to deter the other great powers. Note the use by Canning of the word 'umpire', perhaps an appropriate encapsulation of Britain's role in European diplomacy in the 1820s.

It is one thing to have a giant's strength, but it would be another to use it like a giant. The consciousness of such strength is, undoubtedly, a source of confidence and security; but in the situation in which this country stands, our business is not to seek opportunities of displaying it, but to content ourselves with letting the professors of violent and exaggerated doctrines on both sides feel, that it is not in their interest to convert an umpire into an adversary ... Let us fly to the aid of Portugal, by whomsoever attacked, because it is our duty to do so; and let us cease our interference where that duty ends. We go to Portugal, not to rule, not to dictate, not to prescribe constitutions, but to defend and preserve the independence of an ally. We go to plant the standard of England on the well-known heights of Lisbon. Where that standard is planted, foreign dominion shall not come.

Hansard, 2nd ser., vol. xvi, cols. 367–9, 12 December 1826

document 15

Tory uncertainties after the departure of Lord Liverpool

This document provides a glimpse of a troubled and perplexed political world in the long hiatus between Liverpool's stroke in January and the formation of Canning's government in April 1827. The succession was by no means certain and the contentious issues which Liverpool's presence had held in check, most notably the Catholic emancipation issue, divided old political colleagues. Here one supporter of Canning's claims to succeed Liverpool writes to another about the burning issue of the day. The letter is a good example of informed political gossip and, like many of its ilk, its predictions were largely falsified by subsequent events.

London, 23 February 1827

The two principal speculations are – Canning avowedly head over all – with Robinson sent to lead in the Lords – & then in the event of Canning's clinging (wh. he will in any event be much dispos'd to do) to the F[oreign] Office – Robinson to be First Lord – & Huskisson of the Exchequer. 2nd. speculation. Robinson to be a peer – *First Minister* & First Lord – Huskisson Chancellor of the Exchequer. Other things as they are. This is founded on the notion that in the existing state of matters in the Cabinet there would be as great a difficulty in making some consent to serve under Canning – as it would be to make him serve under them & that this is your only safe compromise. This might be consider'd a patching up *pro tempore* – & indeed it would not have anything very solid in it. Some who speak of this (wh. is a very common speculation) seem to think that Peel & the Duke of Welln. would object to Canning's being Premier – the former on the ground of the Cath. question.

Letter from Lord Bining to Sir Charles Bagot in A. Aspinall (ed.), *The Formation of Canning's Ministry*, Camden Society, 3rd series, vol. lix, 1937, pp. 23–4

document 16

Samuel Bamford on the influence of William Cobbett

Samuel Bamford, a weaver from Middleton, near Manchester, was a leading working-class politician who was twice imprisoned for his radical activities between 1815 and 1821. His story of political activity in Lancashire is both rich in detail and extremely rare. Few working men left such a vivid account. It is a useful corrective to the far larger number of sources which write about working-class activity (whether sympathetically or not) from the outside.

At this time [December 1816] the writings of William Cobbett suddenly became of great authority; they were read on nearly every cottage hearth in the manufacturing districts of South Lancashire, in those of Leicester, Derby and Nottingham; also in many of the Scottish manufacturing towns. Their influence was speedily visible; he directed his readers to the true cause of their sufferings – misgovernment; and to its proper corrective – parliamentary reform. Riots soon became scarce . . .

Instead of riots and destruction of property, Hampden clubs were now established in many of our large towns, and the villages and districts around them; Cobbett's books were printed in a cheap edition form; the labourers read them and thenceforward became deliberate and systematic in their proceedings. Nor were there wanting men of their own class, to encourage and direct the new converts; the Sunday Schools of the preceding thirty years, had produced many working men of sufficient talent to become readers, writers and speakers in the village meetings for parliamentary reform.

Samuel Bamford, *Passages in the Life of a Radical*, Oxford University Press ed., 1984, pp. 13–14

document 17

Cobbett's Address to the Journeymen and Labourers

This is the kind of appeal which Bamford [**doc. 16**] *alleged moved its readers and hearers to dignified but committed protest. Cobbett was no socialist but he had a clear idea of the dignity of labour which he passed on to his readers in direct, vigorous prose.*

As it is the labour of those who toil which makes a country abound in resources, so it is the same class of men, who must, by their arms, secure its safety and uphold its fame. Titles and immense sums of money have been bestowed upon numerous Naval and Military Commanders. Without calling the justice of these in question, we may assert that the victories were obtained by you and your fathers and brothers and sons in co-operation with those Commanders, who, with *your* aid have done great and wonderful things . . .

With this correct idea of your own worth in your minds, with what indignation must you hear yourselves called the Populace, the Rabble, the Mob, the Swinish Multitude; and with what greater indignation, if possible, must you hear the projects of those cool and cruel and insolent men, who, now that you have been, without any fault of yours, brought into a state of misery, propose to narrow the limits of parish relief, to prevent you from marrying in the days of your youth, or to thrust you out to seek your bread in foreign lands, never more to behold your parents and friends?

. . . As to the cause of our present miseries, it is the *enormous amount of the taxes*, which the government compels us to pay for the support of its army, its placemen, its pensioners, etc. and for the payment of the interest of its debt . . . The *remedy* is what we have now to look to, and that remedy consists wholly and solely of such a *reform* in the Commons or People's House of Parliament, as shall give to every payer of *direct taxes* a vote at elections, and as shall cause the Members to be *elected annually*.

Cobbett's Political Register, 2 November 1816, reprinted in G. D. H. Cole and A. W. Filson (eds.), *British Working Class Movements: Select Documents, 1789–1875*, Macmillan, London, 1967 ed., pp. 122–3

document 18

A Slap at Cobbett

The recent resurgence of interest in working-class politics has uncovered a treasure-trove of radical literature which is becoming ever more widely available in reprints and new editions. It must not be forgotten that, though few could rival Cobbett's journalistic abilities, he did not lack for combatants. The following document is almost totally unknown. It shows how his opponents tried to reduce Cobbett's influence among the poor by asserting the impracticality of Cobbett's schemes and the damage their implementation would do to the very folk he was aiming to persuade. Note the author's reference to what would become known as the March of the Blanketeers (Chapter 4). The last sentence refers to Cobbett's early career as a pro-Tory and anti-reformer in the 1790s.

To the MANCHESTER WORKMEN

MY GOOD FRIENDS – Do not believe, that in addressing you, I am not moved by the most sincere and heartfelt interest in your distresses. I can too well conceive, how much you have of late had to struggle against, to keep yourselves, your wives, and families, from the very extremity of suffering – perhaps from sinking under the pressure of the times; but let me beg you to reflect on the absurd and preposterous method that you have been persuaded to adopt for your relief. You have been advised to set off, by thousands, to walk to London, in order to present your Petitions to the Prince Regent. Now, my good Friends, let me first tell you how, and by whom, and for what purposes, this foolish notion has been put into your heads. You are not aware who it is, that is making fools of you, in this manner; still less do you suspect with what view it is done; but I will detect the villain, I will drag him from his hole. It was COBBETT ... it was he who first proposed a scheme which, he knew, must turn all those who listened to it into Vagabonds, or Rioters, or Thieves ... Whether you may be starved to death on the road, or taken up and hanged, he does not care a doit. He would only call you *silly* and *misguided* people, for your pains; but his end would have been answered; he would have made you dance to his fiddle, and pay him for the music too, though it was leading you to the gallows here, and to eternal torment hereafter. For, my Friends, this greedy grasping wretch, after having written for the rich against the poor, till no respectable person would read his writings any longer, is now trying to squeeze the last farthing out of the pockets of the Poor, by writing against the Rich.

Anti-Cobbett or The Weekly Patriotic Paper, vol. i, no. 5, 15 March 1817, pp. 130–1

document 19
The Spa Fields Meeting of December 1816

*This placard advertised one of the most famous of radical meetings. Notice the directness of the language and the concern with economic privation. Contrast both the language and the message of this placard with that of the 'call to arms' [**doc. 20**] and then with that of the Report of the Committee of Secrecy [**doc. 21**].*

ENGLAND
Expects every Man to do his Duty

The Meeting in Spa Fields
Takes Place at 12 o'clock
On Monday, December 2nd. 1816

To receive the answer of the PETITION to the PRINCE REGENT, determined upon at the last meeting held in the same place, and for other important Considerations.

THE PRESENT STATE OF GREAT BRITAIN
Four Millions in Distress !!!
Four Millions Embarrassed !!!
One Million-and-half fear Distress !!!
Half-a-million live in splendid Luxury !!!

Death would now be a relief to Millions –
Arrogance, Folly, and Crimes – have brought affairs to this dread Crisis.

Firmness and Integrity
can only save the Country!!!

State Trials, vol. xxxii, 1817, p. 86

document 20

A Call to Arms

Documents like the following, which was circulated before the Spa Fields Meeting of December 1816 and reprinted in the Committee of Secrecy report, could be used by the authorities to justify legislation which suspended the normal liberties of the subject for protest and peaceable assembly. The tenor of the Report suggests, however, that, although there was indeed a 'project' for 'raising an insurrection' at the end of 1816 the threat which this announcement seems to offer was well under control. Notice the specific targets listed by the author of the handbill.

Britons to Arms!
The whole country waits the signal from London to fly to arms!

haste, break open gunsmiths and other likely places to find arms! run all constables who touch a man of us; no rise of bread; No Regent; no Castlereagh, off with their heads; no placemen, tythes or enclosures; no taxes; no bishops.

Reprinted in *Hansard*, 1st ser, vol. xxxv, 1817, cols. 440–1

document 21
The Report of the Committee of Secrecy, February 1817

This Report followed very similar procedures from those of the Secrecy Committees established by the younger Pitt in the 1790s. It provided abundant evidence of disaffection, sufficient to justify, at least to a majority of MPs, legislation concerned to strengthen public order. The blame, of course, could be laid at the door of hotheads and trouble-makers conveniently known to the authorities. Ordinary Britons could thus be absolved from blame and, indeed, praised for their forbearance in the face of economic hardship.

On a review of the whole it is a great satisfaction to your Committee to observe that, notwithstanding the alarming progress which has been made in the system of secret societies, its success has been confined to the principle [*sic*] manufacturing districts where the distress is more prevalent, and numbers more easily collected; and that even in many of these districts, privations have been borne with exemplary patience and resignation, and the attempts of the disaffected have been disappointed; that few if any of the higher orders or even of the middle class of society, and scarcely any of the agricultural population, have lent themselves to the more violent of these projects. Great allowance must be made for those who, under the pressure of urgent distress, have been led to listen to plausible and confident demagogues, in the expectation of immediate relief. It is to be hoped, that many of those who have engaged, to a certain extent, in the projects of the disaffected, but in whom the principles of moral and religious duty [*sic*] have not been extinguished or perverted by the most profane and miserable sophistry, would withdraw themselves before those projects were pushed to actual insurrection.

Hansard, 1st ser., vol. xxxv, 1817, cols. 446–7

A Radical attack on levels of Taxation

This article, by one of the most gifted of radical jounalists, T. J. Wooler, is in the mainstream of extra-parliamentary opposition. It argues that government taxation policies exaggerate the already wide gulf between rich and poor. Notice the reference to the recent Corn Law as only one of a number of punitive taxes. In Wooler's view, the much-vaunted 'liberties' of the freeborn Englishman had, in fact, been systematically shackled by the corrupt men who ruled Britain in their own interest.

France offers brandies to all the world, at less than *three shillings* a gallon; but an Englishman is not at liberty to drink it, unless he can pay six or seven and twenty shillings a gallon. And if the plenty of the world were to bring its superfluous corn to the British shores, and offer it at *twenty* shillings a quarter, the masters of the freeborn Englishman would insist upon it that he should not have it at a less price than *eighty*. His salt costs him six times what it is worth, as salt . . . his tea pays a hundred per cent duty; in short I am tired of enumerating all his *privileges* . . . the *real* and *only freedom* of an Englishman, is *money* and *money* alone. If rich, what he can *buy* he may have. If great, what he can *take* is his; but your poor free-born Briton is one of the most miserable of human beings. He labours more, and earns less than any other labourer. His skill and enterprize are only equalled by his want and misery – his freedom, is the liberty of seeking his only refuge from calamity – the grave!

The Black Dwarf, 8 December 1819

Radical Freethought in the 1820s

Richard Carlile was a disciple of Tom Paine who took his master's writings several stages further by attacking organised religion as a servile prop to the system of old corruption. He was frequently imprisoned for articles which were widely considered blasphemous and seditious. Though atheism was an important strain in radical political thought at this time, Carlile's work embarrassed many extra-parliamentary radicals who believed that he alienated potential sympathisers in both the middle and the working classes with his trenchantly unfashionable views. Contrast the message here with that offered by Wooler [**doc. 22**].

Since nature has not furnished mankind with Kings, Lords and Priests . . . it follows, that their existence must be the result of good policy in the whole, or of trick in a few of the more cunning and powerful . . . Where you see a rich and powerful aristocracy and priesthood you are sure to find a poor people . . . you cannot shake the power of the aristocracy by any insidious means, it must be done by open attack; and to attack the Priests is to attack the aristocracy at their weakest point. In fact, it is attacking them at all points at once; for the ignorance arising from superstition is the stronghold of all the unjust distinctions, and of all the splendid idlers of society.

Republican, 21 May 1824

document 24

The repeal of the Test and Corporation Acts attacked

*While Catholic emancipation [**doc. 25**] aroused the wider political passions, it would be wrong to think that the long-delayed measure which granted equality in most spheres to Protestant dissenters passed without controversy. Some zealous defenders of the Church of England saw it as a fundamental breach of the constitution.*

. . . a more complete subversion of the principles upon which our Constitution has been founded, we cannot imagine; a more ridiculous, inconsistent, and irrational attempt at argument, is not to be found out of Bedlam; and we grieve to say, that it is not to Lord John Russell, or his supporters, that we apply these epithets; . . . with sincere and poignant grief, we must confess, that they are applicable to those whom we had hoped would have proved themselves the constant and uncompromising defenders of the Established Church.

John Bull, 21 April 1828, p. 124

document 25

Sir Robert Peel concedes Roman Catholic Emancipation

Peel had made his early political reputation not only as an effective minister and administrator but also as a zealous defender of Protestant rights in

117

Ireland – hence the sardonic epithet 'Orange Peel'. The speech from which this document is a brief extract had momentous political consequences both for Peel and the future Conservative party. It ensured the passage of emancipation and it earned Peel the undying hostility of a large proportion of Tory backbenchers. For some, indeed, the collapse of Peel's government in 1846 was a long-delayed and richly-merited retribution for his 'betrayal' in 1829. Note how Peel explains his change of mind. Many of his Tory opponents found his explanation inadequate.

Sir, I approach this subject, almost overpowered by the magnitude of the interests it involves, and by the difficulties with which it is surrounded. I am not unconscious of the degree to which those difficulties are increased by the peculiar situation of him on whom the lot has been cast to propose this measure, and to enforce the expediency of its adoption ... I believe that the time has come when less danger is to be apprehended to the general interests of the empire and to the spiritual and temporal welfare of the Protestant Establishment, in attempting to adjust the Catholic Question, than in allowing it to remain any longer in its present state ... I do not think it was an unnatural or unreasonable struggle. I resign it, in consequence of the conviction that it can be no longer advantageously maintained; from believing that there are not adequate materials or sufficient instruments for its effectual and permanent continuance. I yield, therefore, to a moral necessity which I cannot control, unwilling to push resistance to a point which might endanger the Establishments that I wish to defend.

Hansard, 2nd. ser., vol. xx, 5 March 1829 cols. 728–30

A Provincial Election in 1830

documents 26–28

This election gives the flavour of the hustings when opinion was growing in favour of parliamentary reform. It saw the defeat of Robert Peel's 'high' Tory brother, Jonathan. His letter requesting the electors' continued support [**doc. 26**] *was typical of many sent by retiring members confident of re-election. The attack on him, written anonymously* [**doc. 27**], *makes standard radical charges of nepotism and excessive spending of public money in an embarrassingly* ad hominem *fashion. Peel's defeat was a significant straw in the wind. Norwich, though a constituency in which money frequently changed hands when votes were sought, was one of the largest freemen* *boroughs in the country with an electorate which exceeded 3,000 and thus indicative of the changing state of public opinion. Robert Grant was a Huskissonite and, as such, the target of a campaign mounted by Wellington's government to defeat as many of their former political allies as possible. Grant's victory over Peel [doc. 28] was indicative of the limited support for Wellington in the contested constituencies. The candidate who came top of the poll, Richard Gurney, was a wealthy Whig banker who was reputed to have spent more than £3,000 a year on maintaining his support in the constituency.*

document 26

To the Worthy the Clergy, Freemen and Freeholders of the City of Norwich, 28 June 1830
Gentlemen . . .
I lose not a moment in communicating to you my intention of again soliciting the favour of your suffrages in the honourable and distinguished situation which I now occupy as one of the Representatives of your ancient and populous city.

I refer you to my conduct in Parliament for the fulfilment of the promises I made when first you committed to me the important trust. It has been my earnest desire to merit your confidence and esteem, and to re-deliver that Trust unsullied into your hands. Should I again have the honour of representing you in Parliament, it is my intention steadily to pursue the same line of public policy which I have hitherto adopted, believing it to be best calculated for supporting the real and permanent Interests of the Country . . .

Your most obedient humble servant, Jonathan Peel

document 27

'No Grumbling' to the Independent Electors of the City of Norwich, June 1830

Mr. Peel and his family too, fully understand real and permanent interests, but it is for you to say whether the real and permanent interests he speaks of and is so well acquainted with are in the interests of the country or not.

'A Well Paid Family'

	Per Ann
The Right Hon. R. Peel is a Secretary of State, with a Salary of	£6,000
Mr. W. Peel is under Secretary of State, with a Salary of	2,000
Mr. Lawrence Peel is a Commander for the affairs of India, probably of considerable profit, but no Salary.	
Mr. Dawson, their Brother-in-Law Secretary to the Treasury, with a Salary of	4,000
Besides the following appointments held by their immediate followers	
Mr. Gouldbourn [*sic*], Chancellor of the Exchequer	5,000
Dr. Loyd, Bishop of Oxford, Mr. Peel's private tutor	4,000

Mr. Jonathan Peel, a Young Brother of Mr. Secretary Peel, and Sir Henry Floyd, Mrs. Peel's Brother, Lieut. Colonels in the Army, although we believe neither the one nor the other ever distinguished themselves in the Service of the Country.

Brother Electors – It must be in your memory, that many virtuous attempts to reduce items in the Enormous Taxation, have been made in the present Session of Parliament, and you are hereby informed that Mr. Jonathan Peel uniformly voted for their continuance, and he tells you, that so long as he is your Representative, he will pursue the same policy, yes, and so he has a right, if you again elect him to represent you, after seeing how his interest is identified with the system, and should the Aristocracy demand it, you will have a right to pay double the amount of Taxes which you now pay without grumbling, should Mr. Peel be returned.

document 28

The rapidity with which the Polling proceeded, astonished even the oldest campaigner. The state of the Poll at Six o'Clock will bear us out in this remark: – For

Mr. Gurney	2032
– Grant	1963
– Peel	1699
– Ogle	1560

Majority in favour of Mr. Gurney, 340 – Mr. Grant, 264

The Norwich Election Budget, Containing a Narrative of the Proceedings, Norwich, 1830 and 1831, pp. 10–11, 31, 40–1, copy in British Library

document 29
Wellington misjudges the parliamentary mood

This speech, it is generally agreed, hastened the collapse of Wellington's government. Taken at face value, its assertions were clearly nonsensical at a time of mounting public agitation (Chapter 13). As a way of rallying Tory support, the speech also missed its mark. The speech amounted to a public declaration of ministerial suicide.

He had never read or heard of any measure . . . which could in any degree satisfy his mind that the state of the representation could be improved, or be rendered more satisfactory to the country at large . . . He was fully convinced that the country possessed at the present moment a Legislature which answered all the good purposes of legislation, and this to a greater degree than any Legislature ever had answered in any country whatever. He would go further and say, that the Legislature and the system of representation possessed the full and entire confidence of the country . . . as far as he was concerned, as long as he held any station in the government of the country, he should always feel it his duty to resist such measures [of reform] when proposed by others.

Hansard, 3rd ser., vol. i, 2 November 1830, cols. 52–3

document 30
A hostile view of the political unions

This document encapsulates the distaste felt by many property owners for the direct forms of agitation which the political unions fostered after 1830. Notice the references to 'physical power' and the assertions about the intimidatory tactics of the unions.

Besides the usual machinery of petitions, permanent political associations had already begun to be formed in different parts of the country, for the purpose of organizing large numbers of individuals into one body, to act on the mind of the public around them and press upon the government. These self-constituted organs of popular opinion took the name of Political Unions ... Their objects were, to push on political changes to any extent, by any means; to insist on whatever they chose to demand, as a right which could not be refused without a crime; to repress, by their display of force, any expression, in their neighbourhood, of opinions of an opposite tendency; and to make even the government, which they pretended to be supporting, feel, by their violence, that they existed in order to dictate, not to obey. They did not even conceal the effects which they would produce by their mere physical power, and used language of abuse and intimidation which had no meaning except upon the idea that they were prepared and resolved to extort by force the possession of that power which, in their hands, was to save the country. The great object of all their deliberations was to excite incurable enmity in the middling and lower classes against those who stood above them in the order of society.

Annual Register, 1831, p. 5

document 31
The Prime Minister uses the middle classes as a lever to reform

*This appraisal of the importance of the political unions might usefully be contrasted with that of the Annual Register [**doc. 30**]. Grey's letter is to William IV's private secretary and is designed to inform the King of the importance of middle-class opinion in the government's determination to press ahead with parliamentary reform despite the recent defeat in the Lords (Chapter 16). Behind the bland, respectful tone of the letter there lurked the threat that William IV might have to create peerages in order to coerce Tory opinion in the Upper House. The idea was anathema to the King.*

Earl Grey to Sir H. Taylor, 8 November 1831
These Unions have received a great impulse and extension from the rejection of the Reform Bill; and ... many persons, not otherwise disposed to do so, have been induced to join them for the purpose of promoting that measure. It is also undeniable that the middle classes, who have now shown so praiseworthy an alacrity

in supporting the government, are actuated by an intense and almost unanimous feeling in favour of the measure of reform.

Earl Grey (ed.), *Correspondence of Earl Grey and William IV*, 2 vols, London, 1867, vol. i, pp. 410–11

documents 32 and 33
Sir Robert Inglis and T. B. Macaulay debate the Reform Question

These extracts come from debates in the House of Commons on the second reading of the first Reform Bill. Inglis was MP for Oxford University and a strong opponent of reform. Macaulay was rapidly making a name for himself as a leading writer and orator on the Whig side [doc. 35]. Notice the appeals, respectively, to precedent and to pragmatism. Inglis celebrates a historically ordered entity which represents all of what to him were the important interests. Macaulay similarly rests his case on the enfranchisement of property, not numbers, yet contests the effectiveness of the existing parliamentary system.

document 32

Sir Robert Inglis:
Such, generally speaking, as the House of Commons is now, such it has been for a long succession of years: it is the most complete representation of the interests of the people, which was ever assembled in any age or any country. It is the only constituent body that ever existed, which comprehends within itself those who can urge the wants and defend the claims of the landed, the commercial, the professional classes of the country: those who are bound to uphold the interests of the lower classes, the rights and liberties of the whole people. It is the very absence of symmetry in our elective franchises which admits of the introduction to this House of classes so various.

document 33

T. B. Macaulay:
I oppose Universal Suffrage, because I think it would produce a

destructive revolution . . . We say, and we say justly, that it is not by mere numbers but by property and intelligence that the nation ought to be governed. Yet, saying this, we exclude from all share in the government vast masses of property and intelligence – vast numbers of those who are most interested in preserving tranquillity, and who know best how to preserve it. We do more. We drive over to the sin of revolution those whom we shut out of power.

Monarchy and aristocracy, valuable and useful as I think them, are still useful and valuable as means, and not as ends. The end of government is the happiness of the people; and I do not conceive that, in a country like this, the happiness of the people can be promoted by a form of government in which the middle classes place no confidence, and which exists only because the middle classes have no organ by which to make their sentiments known.

Hansard, 3rd ser., vol. ii, 2 March 1831, cols. 1108–9, 1192–3 and 1199–1200

Reaction to the Reform Bill
document 34

This document derives from the diary of a cabinet minister in Wellington's government of 1828–30. As might be expected, Lord Ellenborough was opposed to parliamentary reform. This extract is useful in indicating an immediate, rather than a considered, judgement on the reform proposals when they were first unveiled before Parliament. Both the surprise and alarm at the radicalism of the Bill and the expectation that it could not pass were typical. The extract neatly conveys both the main strengths and weaknesses of diaries as a historical source.

March 2nd, 1831

The Reform proposed is much more extensive than was expected. Parts of it are very absurd. There was no little laughter as they were detailed. The feeling in the Gallery was against it, as absurd. In the House, Ld. John [Russell] seems to have been little cheered and to have spoken miserably . . . I rather gather . . . that the opponents of Reform are thrown aback by the extent of the proposed change, & alarmed. The feeling, however, is that the Bill cannot pass.

Probably the Ministers wish to be beat upon Reform, & so to go out. How to form any strong Government in their place I know not, but perhaps, for Providence seems always to save us when we are in real danger, the alarm of the influential classes may create a support.

A. Aspinall (ed.), *Three Early Nineteenth-Century Diaries*, Williams and Northgate, London, 1952, pp. 61–2

document 35
An appraisal of Macaulay's debating style

By December 1831, with reform the only important political question, Macaulay had established himself as the pre-eminent debater on the Whig side. This document offers an informed view of his oratory. Debating skill swayed votes in the 1830s, before the days of tight party organisation and the advent of powerful party 'Whips', and Macaulay's skills were important as well as ornamental. E. J. Littleton, from whose diary this extract is taken, was one of the two county MPs for Staffordshire. Like Palmerston, he had been a supporter of Canning and Huskisson in the 1820s and supported the Whigs from November 1830. Unlike Palmerston, however, his ministerial career was brief and inglorious. He served unsuccessfully as Chief Secretary for Ireland in 1833 and 1834.

December 17, 1831
Macaulay made one of those brilliant speeches, his third on the Reform question, which carried the House away in the same furious whirlwind of mixed passions which seemed to seize himself. Never was a more extraordinary compound of deep philosophy, exalted sentiments, and party bitterness, enunciated with a warmth, a vigour, and rapidity inconceivable. The public can collect but little of its character from the papers. It is like the course of a meteor, never to be forgotten by those who have the fortune to see it, but seen by a few.

A. Aspinall (ed.), *Three Early Nineteenth-Century Diaries*, 1952, p. 171

document 36
The political influence of the Established Church

The radical writer John Wade is best remembered for his painstaking researches into the extent of what the radicals called 'Old Corruption'. His most vulnerable target was the Church of England and the analysis which follows seemed particularly relevant during the demonstrations which followed the rejection of the second Reform Bill in October 1831 (Chapter 16). These had a strongly anti-clerical flavour.

The clergy, from superior education, from their wealth and sacred profession, possess greater influence than any other order of men, and all the influence they possess is as subvervient to government as the army or navy, or any other branch of public service. Upon every public occasion the consequence of this influence is apparent. There is no question, however unpopular, which may not obtain countenance by the support of the clergy: being everywhere, and having much to lose, and a great deal to expect, they are always active and zealous in devotion to the interests of those on whom their promotion depends. Hence their anxiety to attract notice at county, corporate, and sessional meetings. Whenever a loyal address is to be obtained, a popular petition opposed, or hard measure carried against the poor, it is almost certain that some reverend rector, very reverend dean, or venerable archdeacon, will make himself conspicuous.

John Wade, *The Extraordinary Black Book*, London, 1831, pp. 20–1

document 37
An attack on authority without understanding

A growing element in the radical critique of the old political system was the argument that those in authority were ignorant of conditions in the rapidly growing industrial areas. This line of reasoning enabled radicals to concentrate on 'lords and parsons', both of whom were in short supply in the early nineteenth-century city. The Poor Man's Advocate was published from Manchester and embraced a wide range of radical causes. Note the reference to 'moral regeneration' in Europe.

There are two classes of men in this country who enjoy the greatest facilities for acquiring, and yet who, in reality, possess the least amount of real knowledge. These are lords and parsons. The one class are set apart to instruct, and the other to rule the people; yet both are lamentably ignorant of the actual state of society. The rank and habits of one class shut them out from that intercourse with the rest of mankind, which is essential to their properly discharging the duty they have undertaken. The supercilious pride and sectarian hostility of the other have rendered them obnoxious rather than acceptable to the people, and both are in equal danger of being swept away by the swelling tide of moral regeneration which has already inundated Europe.

The Poor Man's Advocate, no. 11, 31 March 1832

document 38
The return of the Duke

This document is taken from a provincial newspaper which is trying to analyse the likely consequence of Wellington's resuming office in May 1832. References to the financial implications of the reform crisis were very common both in the London and the provincial press at this time.

We learn that the Duke of Wellington consents to be Premier again! We learn, too, that he will go on with the Reform Bill, and that he proposes to make very little alteration in it!! Parliament will, it is believed, be dissolved immediately, therefore, let the people prepare forthwith. Stocks have fallen one per cent more! ... The greatest alarm is entertained lest the 100,000 men at Birmingham should not be kept from an outbreak. It is felt to be the duty of the Tories to take their post without delay, so that if there should be a conflict between the government and the people, it may not be between the people and Earl Grey ... There is a panic in the city.

Buckinghamshire Gazette, 12 May 1832

document 39
J. W. Croker encounters Manchester working men

This account by a leading Tory writer and intellectual has its unintentionally humorous side, but it is useful to reflect on the cultural chasm which separated the writer from the people he is evidently so reluctant to meet. The incident took place during the 'Days of May' when some, at least, feared imminent revolution.

May 18th, 1832

I remained at Molesey [Surrey], and was surprised at finding that a body of workmen from Manchester (who had been marched up, it seems, to intimidate the King and the new government, but were stopped and ordered back in consequence of the restoration of the Whigs) had quartered themselves in this and the neighbouring villages, and were, like sturdy beggars, insisting on getting food and money. Two of them came to my gate and made some noise, and I could hardly get rid of them. Each carried a small skein of cotton yarn, which they pretended to sell; but when I showed them the absurdity of such a pretence . . . they confessed that they had come up *many thousands* to carry the Reform Bill which was to put down machinery, and enable the poor man to earn a livelihood . . . They wore a kind of workman's uniform – a flannel jacket, trimmed with narrow blue ribbon. One was an Englishman, and civil; the other an Irishman, and very much inclined to riot and rob. But his companion listened to reason, and when he heard that there was a lady dangerously ill in the house, he half forced away his troublesome comrade. I have no doubt that they were part of a body of workmen which have been brought up from Birmingham and Manchester to help the Whigs. I thought it right, however, to apprise Lord Melbourne, Secretary of State for the Home Department, of this migration of the northern hives.

L. J. Jennings (ed.), *The Correspondence and Diaries of J. W. Croker*, 3 vols, London, 1884, vol. ii, pp. 169–70

document 40

The Duke of Wellington considers the likely consequences of reform

Wellington remained defiantly pessimistic about reform up to and beyond the passage of the Reform Act. This letter to a fellow Tory peer, the Duke of Buckingham, indicates his state of mind. Though it is easy to poke fun at predictions which were proved wildly wrong, it is more important to try to understand why they were so widely shared in Tory circles in 1832. For many, the passage of the Reform Act genuinely meant the end of civilisation as they had known it. Less fevered calculations more than a century and a half later still conclude that the Reform Act was one of the most important events in modern political history.

23 June 1832

My dear Duke,
I quite concur with you respecting the symptoms of the times of the last week. They have occasioned a little apprehension in London and elsewhere; but the impression is only temporary. It is not in my power to prevent the consequence of what has been done. The Government of England is destroyed. A Parliament will be returned, by means of which no set of men will be able to conduct the administration of affairs, and to protect the lives and properties of the King's subjects.

I hear the worst accounts of the elections; indeed, I don't believe that gentlemen will be prevailed upon to offer themselves as candidates.

Duke of Buckingham, *Memoirs of the Courts and Cabinets of William the Fourth and Victoria*, 2 vols, London, 1861, vol. i, p. 5

Bibliography

The pace of historical scholarship renders all bibliographies out of date as soon as they are published. However, L. M. Brown & I. R. Christie (eds), *The Bibliography of British History, 1789–1851*, Oxford, 1977, is exhaustive on material published before the mid-1970s. D. Nicholls, *Nineteenth-Century Britain, 1815–1914*, Folkestone, 1978, is what is termed a 'critical bibliography'. This appears to mean that it is more selective, while offering some judgements on the works which are chosen for inclusion. In the nature of things, such judgements are subjective. The Historical Association's *Annual Bibliography* of published works keeps the reader up to date and is easy to follow. Some of the critical judgements offered there can grate but the series deserves to be more widely used.

DOCUMENTS AND CONTEMPORARY SOURCES
Fortunately there is no shortage of good documentary collections for this period. The biggest is A. Aspinall & E. A. Smith (eds), *English Historical Documents*, vol. xi, 1783–1832, London, 1959. See also H. J. Hanham, *The Nineteenth Century Constitution*, 2nd. ed., Cambridge, 1969.

On foreign policy the best collections, with commentary, are H. Temperley & L. M. Penson, *The Foundations of British Foreign Policy from Pitt to Salisbury*, Cambridge, 1938, and K. Bourne, *The Foreign Policy of Victorian England, 1830–1902*, Oxford, 1970. Readers are advised not to be deterred either by the title's eccentric definition of the Victorian period or the book's apparently marginal relevance to the period 1815–32. The first section has some excellent material on Castlereagh and Canning.

Chapters 1 and 2 of Norman Gash, *The Age of Peel*, Arnold, 1968 contain some useful documentary material on religion and on parliamentary reform. The best collection of documents concerned with radicalism, working-class politics and trade unionism remains G. D. H. Cole and A. W. Filson, *British Working Class Movements, 1789–1875*, Macmillan, 1967 ed, though P. Hollis, *Class and Conflict in Nineteenth-Century England, 1815–1850*, Routledge, 1973, is also valuable. See also the Seminar Study by D. G. Wright (**78**).

The political culture of the age ensured a flourishing supply of sophisticated commentators and diarists on the fringes of power who knew their restricted world well and wrote about it brilliantly. Their works offer an excellent quarry for the historian. The commentators and diarists are frequently as unintentionally revealing about themselves and the assumptions they harboured about their inbred society as they are perceptive about their contemporaries. The best for this period are F. Bamford and the Duke of Wellington (eds), *The Journal of Mrs. Arbuthnot*, 1950; A. Aspinall (ed.), *Three Early Nineteenth-Century Diaries*, 1952; H. Maxwell (ed.), *The Creevey Papers*, 1923; L. J. Jennings (ed.), *The Correspondence and Diaries of J. W. Croker*, 3 vols, 1884; L. Strachey and R. Fulford, (eds), *The Greville Memoirs*, 7 vols, 1938; L. Melville, (ed.), *The Huskisson Papers*, 1931; and C. D. Yonge, (ed.), *The Life and Administration of the Second Earl of Liverpool*, 3 vols, 1868.

Diaries of the less privileged are naturally much sparser but a new paperback edition of Samuel Bamford's *Passages in the Life of a Radical*, Oxford University Press, 1984, is well worth consulting, especially for a close and sympathetic view of the Lancashire agitations of 1816–21. A complete two-volume edition edited by H. Duckley was published in 1893. Mary Thale (ed.), *The Autobiography of Francis Place*, Cambridge, 1973, is an interesting statement by one of the great upwardly mobile political organisers and fixers of the age. The radical writers of the period are best examined in the journals referred to in Chapters 4, 5 and 15 but special attention may be drawn to the assiduous researches about 'Old Corruption' published by John Wade as *The Extraordinary Black Book* in 1831. His entertainingly tendentious *British History Chronologically Arranged* (1839) gives a graphic, one-sided account of the reform crisis. If students are in need of an antidote, the yearly introductions to the *Annual Register* rapidly reveal the real sympathies beneath the misleadingly neutral title.

SECONDARY SOURCES: BOOKS

General works
1 Bentley, M., *Politics without Democracy, 1815–1914*, Fontana, 1984.
2 Briggs, A., *The Age of Improvement, 1783–1867*, Longman, revised ed. 1979.

Bibliography

3 Cannon, J. (ed.), *Aristocratic Century*, Cambridge, 1984.
4 Evans, E. J., *The Forging of the Modern State: Early Industrial Britain, 1783–1870*, Longman, 1983.
5 Gash, N., *Aristocracy and People, 1815–1865*, Arnold, 1979.
6 Halévy, E., *The Liberal Awakening, 1815–30*, vol. 2 of his *History of the English People in the Nineteenth Century*, Benn, 1926.
7 Royle, E., *Modern Britain, 1750–1985: A Social History*, Arnold, 1987.

Politics and Parties

8 Brock, W. R., *Lord Liverpool and Liberal Toryism*, 2nd ed., Glasgow, 1967.
9 Cookson, J. E., *Lord Liverpool's Administration, 1815–1822*, Scottish Academic Press, Edinburgh, 1975.
10 Evans, E. J., *Political Parties in Britain, 1783–1867*, Methuen, 1983.
11 Hill, B. W., *British Parliamentary Parties, 1742–1832*, Allen and Unwin, 1985.
12 Mitchell, A., *The Whigs in Opposition*, Oxford, 1967.
13 Moore, D. C., *The Politics of Deference*, Harvester, 1976.
14 Stewart, R., *The Foundation of the Conservative Party, 1830–67*, Longman, 1978.
15 Thorne, R., (ed.), *The History of Parliament, 1790–1820*, 5 vols, Secker and Warburg, 1986.

Biography

16 Bartlett, C. J., *Castlereagh*, Macmillan, 1966.
17 Bourne, K., *Palmerston: The Early Years, 1784–1841*, Allen Lane, 1982.
18 Derry, J. W., *Castlereagh*, Allen Lane, 1976.
19 Gash, N., *Lord Liverpool*, Weidenfeld, 1984.
20 Gash, N., *Mr. Secretary Peel: The Life of Sir Robert Peel to 1830*, 2nd ed., Longman, 1985.
21 Gash, N., *Sir Robert Peel: The Life of Sir Robert Peel after 1830*, 2nd ed., Longman, 1986.
22 Hinde, W., *Canning*, Collins, 1973.
23 Hinde, W., *Castlereagh*, Collins, 1981.
24 Jones, W. D., *Prosperity Robinson: The Life of Viscount Goderich, 1782–1859*, Macmillan, 1967.
25 Jupp, P., *Lord Grenville, 1759–1834*, Oxford, 1985.
26 Prest, J., *Lord John Russell*, Macmillan, 1972.

27 Stewart, R., *Henry Brougham: His Public Career, 1778–1868*, Bodley Head, 1985.
28 Thompson, N., *Wellington after Waterloo*, Routledge, 1986.
29 Trevelyan, G. M., *Lord Grey of the Reform Bill*, Longman, 1920.
30 Ziegler, P., *Melbourne*, Collins, 1976.

Society
31 Cannon, J. (ed.), *The Whig Ascendancy*, Arnold, 1981.
32 Clark, J. C. D., *English Society, 1688–1832*, Cambridge, 1985.
33 Dunbabin, J. P. D., *Rural Discontent in Nineteenth-Century Britain*, Faber, 1974.
34 Emsley, C., *Crime and Society in England, 1750–1900*, Longman, 1987.
35 Glen, R., *Urban Workers in the Early Industrial Revolution*, Croom Helm, 1984.
36 Henriques, U. R. Q., *Before the Welfare State*, Longman, 1979.
37 Hobsbawm, E. J., and Rudé, G. F. E., *Captain Swing*, Pelican ed., 1973.
38 Hunt, E. H., *British Labour History, 1815–1914*, Weidenfeld, 1981.
39 Peacock, A. J., *Bread or Blood*, Gollancz, 1965.
40 Perkin, H. J., *The Origins of Modern English Society, 1780–1880*, Routledge, 1969.
41 Poynter, J. R., *Society and Pauperism*, Routledge, 1969.
42 Price, R., *Labour in British Society*, Croom Helm, 1986.
43 Read, D., *Press and People, 1790–1850*, Arnold, 1961.
44 Rule, J., *The Labouring Classes in Early Industrial England*, Longman, 1986.
45 Stevenson, J., *London in the Age of Reform*, Blackwell, 1977.
46 Stevenson, J., *Popular Disturbances in England, 1700–1870*, Longman, 1979.
47 Taylor, A. (ed.), *The Standard of Living Controversy in the Industrial Revolution*, Methuen, 1975.
48 Thompson, E. P., *The Making of the English Working Class*, Gollancz, 1963.
49 Tranter, N. L., *Population and Society, 1750–1940*, Longman, 1985.
50 Williams, G., *The Merthyr Rising*, Croom Helm, 1978.

Trade, Economics and Finance
51 Deane, P. and Cole, W. A., *British Economic Growth, 1688–1959*, 2nd ed., Cambridge, 1969.

52 Floud, R. and McCloskey, D. (eds), *The Economic History of Britain since 1700*, 2 vols, Cambridge, 1981.

53 Gordon, B., *Economic Doctrine and Tory Liberalism, 1824–30*, Macmillan, 1979.

54 Gordon, B., *Political Economy in Parliament, 1819–23*, Macmillan, 1976.

55 Hilton, B., *Corn, Cash, Commerce: The Economic Policies of the Tory Governments, 1815–1830*, Oxford, 1977.

56 Thompson, N. W., *The People's Science: The Popular Political Economy of Exploitation and Crisis, 1816–1834*, Cambridge, 1984.

Religion

57 Bossy, J., *The English Catholic Community, 1570–1850*, Darton, Longman and Todd, 1975.

58 Hempton, D., *Methodism and Politics in British Society, 1780–1850*, Hutchinson, 1984.

59 Machin, G. I. T., *The Catholic Question in English Politics, 1820–30*, Oxford, 1964.

60 Royle, E., *Radical Politics, 1790–1900: Religion and Unbelief*, Longman, 1971.

Foreign Policy

61 Chamberlain, M. E., *British Foreign Policy in the Age of Palmerston*, Longman, 1980.

62 Hayes, P., *The Nineteenth Century, 1814–80*, A. and C. Black, 1975.

63 Hyam, R., *Britain's Imperial Century, 1815–1914*, Batsford, 1976.

64 Seton-Watson, R. W., *Britain in Europe, 1789–1914*, Cambridge, 1937.

Radical Politics

65 Belchem, J., *'Orator' Hunt*, Clarendon, 1985.

66 Dinwiddy, J. R., *From Luddism to the Reform Act*, Blackwell, 1986.

67 Flick, C., *The Birmingham Political Union, 1830–39*, Dawson, 1978.

68 Goodwin, A., *The Friends of Liberty*, Manchester University Press, 1978.

69 Green, D., *Great Cobbett, The Noblest Agitator*, Oxford, 1983.

70 Prothero, I., *Artisans and Politics in Nineteenth-Century London*, Dawson, 1979.

71 Royle, E. and Walvin, J., *English Radicals and Reformers, 1760–1848*, Harvester, 1982.
72 Thomis, M. I. and Holt, P., *Threats of Revolution in Britain, 1789–1848*, Macmillan, 1977.
73 Ward, J. T., (ed.), *Popular Movements, 1830–50*, Macmillan, 1970.

Parliamentary Reform
74 Brock, M., *The Great Reform Act*, Hutchinson, 1973.
75 Butler, J. R. M., *The Passing of the Reform Bill*, Cass ed., 1914.
76 Cannon, J., *Parliamentary Reform, 1640–1832*, 2nd ed., Cambridge, 1980.
77 Evans, E. J., *The Great Reform Act*, Methuen, 1983.
78 Wright, D. G., *Democracy and Reform, 1815–1885*, Longman, 1970.

SECONDARY SOURCES: ARTICLES
The following abbreviations are used:

HJ	*Historical Journal*
JMH	*Journal of Modern History*
EHR	*English Historical Review*
Econ. HR	*Economic History Review*
P & P	*Past and Present*
ESR	*European Studies Review*
PH	*Parliamentary History*

Politics and Parties
79 Clark, J. C. D., 'A General Theory of Party, Opposition and Government, 1688–1832', *HJ*, xxiii, 1980, pp. 295–325.
80 Flick, C., 'The Fall of Wellington's Government', *JMH*, xxxvii, 1965, pp. 62–71.
81 Fraser, P., 'Party Voting in the House of Commons, 1812–27', *EHR*, xcviii, 1983, pp. 763–84.
82 O'Gorman, F., 'Electoral Deference in "Unreformed" England, 1760–1832', *JMH*, lvi, 1984, pp. 391–427.
83 O'Gorman, F., 'Party Politics in the Early Nineteenth Century, 1812–32', *EHR*, cii, 1987, pp. 63–84.

Society
84 Flinn, M. W., 'Trends in Real Wages', *Econ. HR*, 2nd ser., xxvii, 1974, pp. 395–413.

85 Lindert, P. H. and Williamson, J. G., 'English Workers' Living Standards during the Industrial Revolution: A New Look', *Econ. HR*, 2nd ser., xxxvi, 1983, pp. 1–25.

86 Gatrell, V. A. C., 'Labour, Power and the Size of Firms in Lancashire Cotton in the second quarter of the nineteenth century', *Econ. HR*, 2nd ser., xxx, 1977, pp. 95–139.

Religion

87 Davis, R. W., 'The Tories, the Whigs and Catholic Emancipation, 1827–9', *EHR*, xcvii, 1982, pp. 89–98.

88 Evans, E. J., 'Some Reasons for the Growth of Rural Anti-Clericalism in England, c. 1750–1830', *P & P*, lxvi, 1975, pp. 84–109.

89 Evans, E. J., 'The Church in Danger? Anti-Clericalism in Nineteenth-Century England', *ESR*, xiii, 1983, pp. 201–23.

90 Machin, G. I. T., 'Canning, Wellington and the Catholic Question, 1827–29', *EHR*, xcvii, 1984, pp. 94–100.

91 Machin, G. I. T., 'Resistance to the Repeal of the Test and Corporation Acts', *HJ*, xxii, 1979, pp. 115–39.

Parliamentary Reform

92 Davis, R. W., 'Toryism to Tamworth: The Triumph of Reform, 1827–35', *Albion*, xii, 1980, pp. 132–46.

93 McCord, N., 'Some Difficulties of Parliamentary Reform', *HJ*, x, 1967, pp. 376–90.

94 Moore, D. C., 'Concession or Cure: The Sociological Premises of the First Reform Act', *HJ*, ix, 1966, pp. 39–59.

95 Phillips, J. A., 'The Many Faces of Reform: The Reform Bill and the Electorate', *PH*, i, 1982, pp. 115–35.

96 Milton-Smith, J., 'Earl Grey's Cabinet and the Objects of Parliamentary Reform', *HJ*, xv, 1972, pp. 55–74.

Index